DICKENS IN FRANCE

*Selected pieces by Charles Dickens
on France and the French*

In Print

Foreword © 1996 Edward G. Preston

This selection © 1996 In Print Publishing Ltd

British Library Cataloguing in Publication Data: a catalogue record for this book is available from the British Library.

ISBN 1 873047 76 2

Cover design by Russell Townsend
Typeset by MC Typeset Ltd
Printed by Athenaeum Press Ltd

The Uncommercial Traveller comprises pieces first published in *All the Year Round*. It first appeared in 1860 and several subsequent editions, culminating in that of 1890 which completed the volume as we now know it. *Reprinted Pieces* is a collection of contributions to *Household Words*, and was published in its current form in 1868. *Pictures from Italy* was first published serially in the *Daily News*, and subsequently edited into volume form by Dickens: the edition followed here is that of 1867–68, corrected by the author. The extracted correspondence published in this selection follows the Nonesuch edition of *The Letters of Charles Dickens*, edited by Walter Dexter, The Nonesuch Press, London, 1938.

This selection first published in 1996 by
In Print Publishing Ltd, 9 Beaufort Terrace, Brighton BN2 2SU, UK. Tel: (01273) 682836. Fax: (01273) 620958.

Contents

Dickens crossing the Channel – cartoon by Gill

Foreword

Whilst in several of Dickens's novels we can find references to France and the French, as for example in *Our Mutual Friend*, and indeed whole scenes set there in *Little Dorrit* and *Dombey and Son*, apart from these and *A Tale of Two Cities*, centred upon revolutionary France, it is really to Dickens's shorter, and usually lesser-known writing that we need to turn to discover the true depth of his knowledge of the subject.

This book contains a selection of such writings, placing them conveniently in a handy volume to which the reader can turn both for information regarding French life at that time, travel through France, and much topographical material, couched in typical Dickensian humour.

Many expressions coined by Dickens have passed into our everyday language, and are quoted regularly without a thought being given to their origin. There are also phrases and pithy descriptions which, because they have not become commonplace, are so much the more delightful when discovered, or re-discovered. Some of these have an added charm scattered amongst this selection of his writings about France. My own particular favourite is to be found in *Our French Watering-Place* (pp 80–103) where, in conversation with a French traveller, in anticipation of their journey across the English Channel, Dickens is asked whether he ever suffers from travel sickness. He answers, 'Sir, your servant is always sick

[5]

when it is possible to be so.' The Frenchman demon-
strates his one-upmanship by responding, 'Ah, Heaven,
but I am always sick, even when it is *im*possible to be so.'

Dickens's knowledge of France and the French was
extensive through experience. In a letter to his biographer
John Forster dated 1st November 1843, he intimated his
plans to travel on the continent, and the following year
paid the first of many visits to France. His writings about
this first trip appeared in the small volume entitled
Pictures from Italy, and the passages included here are
most relevant (pp 11–46). He developed a real love for
France and in particular that corner of northern France
around Boulogne which, as the title *Our French Watering-
Place* implies, became a place of frequent sojourning.
A detailed study of his visits there has been carefully
recorded in *De Boulogne à Condette* by Janine Watrin for
those who wish to study this aspect further.

Several extracts from Dickens's letters from France
have wisely been included in *Dickens in France* (pp
116–132) to whet the appetite for the extensive collection
to be found in the Pilgrim Edition of the *Letters of Charles
Dickens*. Dickens became fluent both in speaking and
writing French, and was favourably impressed by many
things French, although he was as open about revealing
errors and corruption in France as he was about revealing
them in his own land. Thus we find this typical comment
in *A Flight* (pp 62–79) which is reminiscent of his
objection to the puffed-up importance of beadles as
revealed through Mr Bumble in *Oliver Twist*: 'Now, I
tread upon French ground, and am greeted by the three

charming words, Liberty, Equality, Fraternity, painted up (in letters a little too thin for their height) on the Custom-house wall – also by the sight of large cocked hats, without which demonstrative head-gear nothing of a public nature can be done upon this soil.'

Always having an observer's eye, nothing went unnoticed by him, neither was it wasted on him. In these selected non-fictional though far from prosaic writings, we can also see the embryo of later novel material. Again I quote from *A Flight* – a descriptive piece about high-speed travel, in which in a light-hearted way, and by attributing descriptive names to his fellow passengers, he gives a full picture. Thus from the views of the one he names Monied Interest we can detect the germ of Mr Podsnap who appeared a few years later in *Our Mutual Friend*. 'Monied Interest has come into my carriage. Says the manner of refreshing is "not bad", but considers it French. Admits great dexterity and politeness in the attendants. Thinks a decimal currency may have something to do with their despatch in settling accounts, and don't know but what it's sensible and convenient. Adds, however, as a general protest, that they're a revolutionary people – and always at it.'

There is a freshness about these writings, particularly being brought together in this way, which, despite their age, and the changes which have ensued in the century-and-a-half since they were first penned, gives them a particular relevance to today's reader.

Most of the articles in this book have been selected from what now appear as *The Uncommercial Traveller* and

Reprinted Pieces, although originally they appeared as separate pieces in journals (see the copyright page of this volume). The reader is supplied with all the information required to trace the source material by the helpful notes at the heading of each item chosen.

Edward G. Preston
Honorary General Secretary
The Dickens Fellowship

Publishers' acknowledgments

The publishers are very grateful to Professor Philip Collins, Dr David Parker, and Edward G. Preston for their advice, to the Dickens House Museum for providing research facilities, and to Edward G. Preston for his contribution of the Foreword. The final selection of contents and any errors or omissions are entirely the responsibility of the publishers.

DICKENS IN FRANCE

GOING THROUGH FRANCE

(from Pictures from Italy)

'This book is made as accessible as possible, because it would be a great pleasure to me if I could hope, through its means, to compare impressions with some among the multitudes who will hereafter visit the scenes described with interest and delight.' In the summer of 1844, Dickens and his family set off on a tour of France and Italy. His memories of the places he visited and the people he met are recorded in Pictures from Italy. Here, we reprint the opening sections of the book which relate to his travels through France.

On a fine Sunday morning in the Midsummer time and weather of eighteen hundred and forty-four, it was, my good friend, when – don't be alarmed; not when two travellers might have been observed slowly making their way over that picturesque and broken ground by which the first chapter of a Middle Age novel is usually attained – but when an English travelling-carriage of considerable proportions, fresh from the shady halls of the Pantechnicon near Belgrave Square, London, was observed (by a very small French soldier; for I saw him look at it) to issue from the gate of the Hôtel Meurice in the Rue Rivoli at Paris.

I am no more bound to explain why the English

family travelling by this carriage, inside and out, should be starting for Italy on a Sunday morning, of all good days in the week, than I am to assign a reason for all the little men in France being soldiers, and all the big men postilions; which is the invariable rule. But, they had some sort of reason for what they did, I have no doubt; and their reason for being there at all, was, as you know, that they were going to live in fair Genoa for a year; and that the head of the family purposed, in that space of time, to stroll about, wherever his restless humour carried him.

And it would have been small comfort to me to have explained to the population of Paris generally, that I was that Head and Chief; and not the radiant embodiment of good humour who sat beside me in the person of a French Courier – best of servants and most beaming of men! Truth to say, he looked a great deal more patriarchal than I, who, in the shadow of his portly presence, dwindled down to no account at all.

There was, of course, very little in the aspect of Paris – as we rattled near the dismal Morgue and over the Pont Neuf – to reproach us for our Sunday travelling. The wine-shops (every second house) were driving a roaring trade; awnings were spreading, and chairs and tables arranging, outside the cafés, preparatory to the eating of ices, and drinking

[12]

of cool liquids, later in the day; shoe-blacks were busy on the bridges; shops were open; carts and waggons clattered to and fro; the narrow, up-hill, funnel-like streets across the River, were so many dense perspectives of crowd and bustle, particoloured night-caps, tobacco-pipes, blouses, large boots, and shaggy heads of hair; nothing at that hour denoted a day of rest, unless it were the appearance, here and there, of a family pleasure-party, crammed into a bulky old lumbering cab; or of some contemplative holiday-maker in the freest and easiest dishabille, leaning out of a low garret window, watching the drying of his newly polished shoes on the little parapet outside (if a gentleman), or the airing of her stockings in the sun (if a lady), with calm anticipation.

Once clear of the never-to-be-forgotten-or-forgiven pavement which surrounds Paris, the first three days of travelling towards Marseilles are quiet and monotonous enough. To Sens. To Avallon. To Chalons. A sketch of one day's proceedings is a sketch of all three; and here it is.

We have four horses, and one postilion, who has a very long whip and drives his team, something like the Courier of Saint Petersburgh in the circle at Astley's or Franconi's: only he sits his own horse instead of standing on him. The immense jack-boots worn by these postilions, are sometimes a

century or two old; and are so ludicrously disprop-
ortionate to the wearer's foot, that the spur, which
is put where his own heel comes, is generally
halfway up the leg of the boots. The man often
comes out of the stable-yard, with his whip in his
hand and his shoes on, and brings out, in both
hands, one boot at a time, which he plants on the
ground by the side of his horse, with great gravity,
until everything is ready. When it is – and oh
Heaven! the noise they make about it! – he gets into
the boots, shoes and all, or is hoisted into them by a
couple of friends; adjusts the rope harness, embos-
sed by the labours of innumerable pigeons in the
stables; makes all the horses kick and plunge;
cracks his whip like a madman; shouts 'En route –
Hi!' and away we go. He is sure to have a contest
with his horse before we have gone very far; and
then he calls him a Thief, and a Brigand, and a Pig,
and what not; and beats him about the head as if he
were made of wood.

There is little more than one variety in the
appearance of the country, for the first two days.
From a dreary plain, to an interminable avenue,
and from an interminable avenue to a dreary plain
again. Plenty of vines there are in the open fields,
but of a short low kind, and not trained in festoons,
but about straight sticks. Beggars innumerable
there are, everywhere; but an extraordinarily scanty

population, and fewer children than I ever encountered. I don't believe we saw a hundred children
between Paris and Chalons. Queer old towns, draw-
bridged and walled: with odd towers at the angles,
like grotesque faces, as if the wall had put a mask
on, and were staring down into the moat; other
strange little towers, in gardens and fields, and
down lanes, and in farm-yards: all alone, and always
round, with a peaked roof, and never used for any
purpose at all; ruinous buildings of all sorts; sometimes an hôtel de ville, sometimes a guard-house,
sometimes a dwelling-house, sometimes a château
with a rank garden, prolific in dandelion, and
watched over by extinguisher-topped turrets, and
blink-eyed little casements; are the standard objects, repeated over and over again. Sometimes we
pass a village inn, with a crumbling wall belonging
to it, and a perfect town of out-houses; and painted
over the gateway, 'Stabling for Sixty Horses;' as
indeed there might be stabling for sixty score, were
there any horses to be stabled there, or anybody
resting there, or anything stirring about the place
but a dangling bush, indicative of the wine inside:
which flutters idly in the wind, in lazy keeping with
everything else, and certainly is never in a green old
age, though always so old as to be dropping to
pieces. And all day long, strange little narrow
waggons, in strings of six or eight, bringing cheese

[15]

from Switzerland, and frequently in charge, the whole line, of one man, or even boy – and he very often asleep in the foremost cart – come jingling past: the horses drowsily ringing the bells upon their harness, and looking as if they thought (no doubt they do) their great blue woolly furniture, of immense weight and thickness, with a pair of grotesque horns growing out of the collar, very much too warm for the Midsummer weather.

Then, there is the Diligence, twice or thrice a-day; with the dusty outsides in blue frocks, like butchers; and the insides in white night-caps; and its cabriolet head on the roof, nodding and shaking, like an idiot's head; and its Young-France passengers staring out of window, with beards down to their waists, and blue spectacles awfully shading their warlike eyes, and very big sticks clenched in their National grasp. Also the Malle Poste, with only a couple of passengers, tearing along at a real good dare-devil pace, and out of sight in no time. Steady old Curés come jolting past, now and then, in such ramshackle, rusty, musty, clattering coaches as no Englishman would believe in; and bony women dawdle about in solitary places, holding cows by ropes while they feed, or digging and hoeing or doing field-work or a more laborious kind, or representing real shepherdesses with their flocks – to obtain an adequate idea of which pursuit

[16]

and its followers, in any country, it is only necessary to take any pastoral poem, or picture, and imagine to yourself whatever is most exquisitely and widely unlike the descriptions therein contained.

You have been travelling along, stupidly enough, as you generally do in the last stage of the day; and the ninety-six bells upon the horses – twenty-four apiece – have been ringing sleepily in your ears for half an hour or so; and it has become a very jog-trot, monotonous, tiresome sort of business; and you have been thinking deeply about the dinner you will have at the next stage; when, down at the end of the long avenue of trees through which you are travelling, the first indication of a town appears, in the shape of some straggling cottages: and the carriage begins to rattle and roll over a horribly uneven pavement. As if the equipage were a great firework, and the mere sight of a smoking cottage chimney had lighted it, instantly it begins to crack and splutter, as if the very devil were in it. Crack, crack, crack, crack. Crack-crack-crack-crack. Crick-crack. Crick-crack. Helo! Hola! Vite! Voleur! Brigand! Hi hi hi! En r-r-r-r-route! Whip, wheels, driver, stones, beggars, children, crack, crack, crack; helo! hola! charité pour l'amour de Dieu! crick-crack-crick-crack; crick, crick, crick; bump, jolt, crack, bump, crick-crack; round the corner, up the narrow street, down the paved hill and on

[17]

the other side; in the gutter; bump, bump; jolt, jog, crick, crick, crick; crack, crack, crack; into the shop-windows on the left-hand side of the street, preliminary to a sweeping turn into the wooden archway on the right; rumble, rumble, rumble; clatter, clatter, clatter; crick, crick, crick; and here we are in the yard of the Hôtel de l'Ecu d'Or; used up, gone out, smoking, spent, exhausted; but sometimes making a false start unexpectedly, with nothing coming of it – like a firework to the last!

The landlady of the Hôtel de l'Ecu d'Or is here; and the landlord of the Hôtel de l'Ecu d'Or is here; and the femme de chambre of the Hôtel de l'Ecu d'Or is here; and a gentleman in a glazed cap, with a red beard like a bosom friend, who is staying at the Hôtel de l'Ecu d'Or, is here; and Monsieur le Curé is walking up and down in a corner of the yard by himself, with a shovel hat upon his head, and a black gown on his back, and a book in one hand, and an umbrella in the other; and everybody, except Monsieur le Curé, is open-mouthed and open-eyed, for the opening of the carriage-door. The landlord of the Hôtel de l'Ecu d'Or, dotes to that extent upon the Courier, that he can hardly wait for his coming down from the box, but embraces his very legs and boot-heels as he descends. 'My Courier! My brave Courier! My friend! My brother!' The landlady loves him, the femme de chambre blesses him, the garçon worships him. The Courier asks if his letter has been received? It has, it has. Are the rooms prepared? They are, they are. The best rooms for my noble Courier. The rooms of state for my gallant Courier; the whole house is at the service of my best of friends! He keeps his hand upon the carriage-door, and asks some other question to enhance the expectation. He carries a green leathern purse outside his coat, suspended by a belt. The idlers look at it; one touches it. It is full of five-franc pieces. Murmurs of admiration are heard among the boys. The landlord falls upon the Courier's neck, and folds him to his breast. He is so much fatter than he was, he says! He looks so rosy and so well!

The door is opened. Breathless expectation. The lady of the family gets out. Ah sweet lady! Beautiful lady! The sister of the lady of the family gets out. Great Heaven, Ma'amselle is charming! First little boy gets out. Ah, what a beautiful little boy! First little girl gets out. Oh, but this is an enchanting child! Second little girl gets out. The landlady, yielding to the finest impulse of our common nature, catches her up in her arms! Second little boy gets out. Oh, the sweet boy! Oh, the tender little family! The baby is handed out. Angelic baby! The baby has topped everything. All the rapture is expended on the baby! Then the two nurses tumble out; and the enthusiasm swelling into madness, the whole family are swept up-stairs as on a cloud; while the idlers press about the carriage, and look into it, and walk round it, and touch it. For it is something to touch a carriage that has held so many people. It is a legacy to leave one's children.

The rooms are on the first floor, except the nursery for the night, which is a great rambling chamber, with four or five beds in it: through a dark passage, up two steps, down four, past a pump, across a balcony, and next door to the stable. The other sleeping apartments are large and lofty; each with two small bedsteads, tastefully hung, like the windows, with red and white drapery. The sitting-room is famous. Dinner is already laid in it for three; and the napkins are folded in cocked-hat fashion. The doors are of red tile. There are no carpets, and not much furniture to speak of; but there is abundance of looking-glass, and there are large vases under glass shades, filled with artificial flowers; and there are plenty of clocks. The whole party are in motion. The brave Courier, in particular, is everywhere: looking after the beds, having wine poured down his throat by his dear brother the landlord, and picking up green cucumbers – always cucumbers; Heaven knows where he gets them – with which he walks about, one in each hand, like truncheons.

[20]

Dinner is announced. There is very thin soup; there are very large loaves – one apiece; a fish; four dishes afterwards; some poultry afterwards; a dessert afterwards; and no lack of wine. There is not much in the dishes; but they are very good, and always ready instantly. When it is nearly dark, the brave Courier, having eaten the two cucumbers, sliced up in the contents of a pretty large decanter of oil, and another of vinegar, emerges from his retreat below, and proposes a visit to the Cathedral, whose massive tower frowns down upon the court-yard of the inn. Off we go; and very solemn and grand it is, in the dim light: so dim at last, that the polite, old, lanthorn-jawed Sacristan has a feeble little bit of candle in his hand, to grope among the tombs with – and looks among the grim columns, very like a lost ghost who is searching for his own.

Underneath the balcony, when we return, the inferior servants of the inn are supping in the open air, at a great table; the dish, a stew of meat and vegetables, smoking hot, and served in the iron cauldron it was boiled in. They have a pitcher of thin wine, and are very merry; merrier than the gentleman with the red beard, who is playing billiards in the light room on the left of the yard, where shadows, with cues in their hands, and cigars in their mouths, cross and recross the window, constantly. Still the thin Curé walks up and down

[21]

alone, with his book and umbrella. And there he walks, and there the billiard-balls rattle, long after we are fast asleep.

We are astir at six next morning. It is a delightful day, shaming yesterday's mud upon the carriage, if anything could shame a carriage, in a land where carriages are never cleaned. Everybody is brisk; and as we finish breakfast, the horses come jingling into the yard from the Post-house. Everything taken out of the carriage is put back again. The brave Courier announces that all is ready, after walking into every room, and looking all around it, to be certain that nothing is left behind. Everybody gets in. Everybody connected with the Hôtel de l'Ecu d'Or is again enchanted. The brave Courier runs into the house for a parcel containing cold fowl, sliced ham, bread and biscuits, for lunch; hands it into the coach; and runs back again.

What has he got in his hand now? More cucumbers? No. A long strip of paper. It's the bill.

The brave Courier has two belts on, this morning: one supporting the purse: another, a mighty good sort of leathern bottle, filled to the throat with the best light Bordeaux wine in the house. He never pays the bill till this bottle is full. Then he disputes it.

He disputes it now, violently. He is still the landlord's brother, but by another father or mother.

[22]

He is not so nearly related to him as he was last night. The landlord scratches his head. The brave Courier points to certain figures in the bill, and intimates that if they remain there, the Hôtel de l'Ecu d'Or is thenceforth and for ever an hôtel de l'Ecu de cuivre. The landlord goes into a little counting-house. The brave Courier follows, forces the bill and a pen into his hand, and talks more rapidly than ever. The landlord takes the pen. The Courier smiles. The landlord makes an alteration. The Courier cuts a joke. The landlord is affectionate, but not weakly so. He bears it like a man. He shakes hands with his brave brother, but he don't hug him. Still, he loves his brother; for he knows that he will be returning that way, one of these fine days, with another family, and he foresees that his heart will yearn towards him again. The brave Courier traverses all round the carriage once, looks at the drag, inspects the wheels, jumps up, gives the word, and away we go!

It is market morning. The market is held in the little square outside in front of the Cathedral. It is crowded with men and women in blue, in red, in green, in white; with canvassed stalls; and fluttering merchandise. The country people are grouped about, with their clean baskets before them. Here, the lace-sellers; there, the butter and egg-sellers; there, the fruit-sellers; there, the shoe-makers. The whole

[23]

place looks as if it were the stage of some great theatre, and the curtain had just run up, for a picturesque ballet. And there is the Cathedral to boot; scene-like: all grim, and swarthy, and mouldering, and cold: just splashing the pavement in one place with faint purple drops, as the morning sun, entering by a little window on the eastern side, struggles through some stained glass panes, on the western.

In five minutes we have passed the iron cross, with a little ragged kneeling-place of turf before it, in the outskirts of the town; and are again upon the road.

LYONS, THE RHONE, AND THE GOBLIN OF AVIGNON

Chalons is a fair resting-place, in right of its good inn on the bank of the river, and the little steam-boats, gay with green and red paint, that come and go upon it: which make up a pleasant and refreshing scene, after the dusty roads. But, unless you would like to dwell on an enormous plain, with jagged rows of irregular poplars on it, that look in the distance like so many combs with broken teeth: and unless you would like to pass your life without the possibility of going up-hill, or going up anything but stairs: you would hardly approve of Chalons as a place of residence.

[24]

You would probably like it better, however, than Lyons: which you may reach, if you will, in one of the before-mentioned steamboats in eight hours.

What a city Lyons is! Talk about people feeling, at certain unlucky times, as if they had tumbled from the clouds! Here is a whole town that is tumbled, anyhow, out of the sky; having been first caught up, like other stones that tumble down from that region, out of fens and barren places, dismal to behold! The two great streets through which the two great rivers dash, and all the little streets whose name is Legion, were scorching, blistering, and sweltering. The houses, high and vast, dirty to excess, rotten as old cheeses, and as thickly peopled. All up the hills that hem the city in, these houses swarm; and the mites inside were lolling out of the windows, and drying their ragged clothes on poles, and crawling in and out at the doors, and coming out to pant and gasp upon the pavement, and creeping in and out among huge piles and bales of fusty, musty, stifling goods; and living, or rather not dying till their time should come, in an exhausted receiver. Every manufacturing town, melted into one, would hardly convey an impression of Lyons as it presented itself to me: for all the undrained, unscavengered qualities of a foreign town, seemed grafted, there, upon the native miseries of a manufacturing one; and it bears such fruit

[25]

as I would go some miles out of my way to avoid encountering again.

In the cool of the evening: or rather in the faded heat of the day: we went to see the Cathedral, where divers old women, and a few dogs, were engaged in contemplation. There was no difference, in point of cleanliness, between its stone pavement and that of the streets; and there was a wax saint, in a little box like a berth aboard ship, with a glass front to it, whom Madame Tussaud would have nothing to say to, on any terms, and which even Westminster Abbey might be ashamed of. If you would know all about the architecture of this church, or any other, its dates, dimensions, endowments, and history, is it not written in Mr. Murray's Guide-Book, and may you not read it there, with thanks to him, as I did!

For this reason, I should abstain from mentioning the curious clocks in Lyons Cathedral, if it were not for a small mistake I made, in connection with that piece of mechanism. The keeper of the church was very anxious it should be shown; partly for the honour of the establishment and the town; and partly, perhaps, because of his deriving a percentage from the additional consideration. However that may be, it was set in motion, and thereupon a host of little doors flew open, and innumerable little figures staggered out of them, and jerked them-

[26]

selves back again, with that special unsteadiness of purpose, and hitching in the gait, which usually attaches to figures that are moved by clock-work. Meanwhile, the Sacristan stood explaining these wonders, and pointing them out, severally, with a wand. There was a centre puppet of the Virgin Mary; and close to her, a small pigeon-hole, out of which another and a very ill-looking puppet made one of the most sudden plunges I ever saw accomplished: instantly flopping back again at sight of her, and banging his little door violently after him. Taking this to be emblematic of the victory over Sin and Death, and not at all unwilling to show that I perfectly understood the subject, in anticipation of the showman, I rashly said, 'Aha! The Evil Spirit. To be sure. He is very soon disposed of.' 'Pardon, Monsieur,' said the Sacristan, with a polite motion of his hand towards the little door, as if introducing somebody – 'The Angel Gabriel!'

Soon after daybreak next morning, we were steaming down the Arrowy Rhone, at the rate of twenty miles an hour, in a very dirty vessel full of merchandise, and with only three or four other passengers for our companions: among them, the most remarkable was a silly, old, meek-faced, garlic-eating, immeasurably polite Chevalier, with a dirty scrap of red ribbon hanging at his button-hole, as if he had tied it there to remind himself of something; as Tom Noddy, in the farce, ties knots in his pocket-handkerchief.

For the last two days, we had seen great sullen hills, the first indications of the Alps, towering in the distance. Now, we were rushing on beside them: sometimes close beside them: sometimes with an intervening slope, covered with vineyards. Villages and small towns hanging in mid-air, with great woods of olives seen through the light open towers of their churches, and clouds moving slowly on, upon the steep acclivity behind them; ruined castles perched on every eminence; and scattered houses in the clefts and gullies of the hills; made it very beautiful. The great height of these, too, making the buildings look so tiny, that they had all the charm of elegant models; their excessive white-ness, as contrasted with the brown rocks, or the sombre, deep, dull, heavy green of the olive-tree; and the puny size, and little slow walk of the Lilliputian men and women on the bank; made a charming picture. There were ferries out of num-ber, too; bridges; the famous Pont d'Esprit, with I don't know how many arches; towns where memor-able wines are made; Vallence, where Napoleon studied; and the noble river, bringing at every winding turn, new beauties into view.

There lay before us, that same afternoon, the broken bridge of Avignon, and all the city baking in

[28]

the sun; yet with an under-done-pie-crust, battlemented wall, that never will be brown, though it bake for centuries.

The grapes were hanging in clusters in the streets, and the brilliant Oleander was in full bloom everywhere. The streets are old and very narrow, but tolerably clean, and shaded by awnings stretched from house to house. Bright stuffs and handkerchiefs, curiosities, ancient frames of carved wood, old chairs, ghostly tables, saints, virgins, angels, and staring daubs of portraits, being exposed for sale beneath, it was very quaint and lively. All this was much set off, too, by the glimpses one caught, through a rusty gate standing ajar, of quiet sleepy court-yards, having stately old houses within, as silent as tombs. It was all very like one of the descriptions in the Arabian Nights. The three one-eyed Calenders might have knocked at any one of those doors till the street rang again, and the porter who persisted in asking questions – the man who had the delicious purchases put into his basket in the morning – might have opened it quite naturally.

After breakfast next morning, we sallied forth to see the lions. Such a delicious breeze was blowing in, from the north, as made the walk delightful: though the pavement-stones, and stones of the walls and houses, were far too hot to have a hand laid on them comfortably.

[29]

We went, first of all, up to a rocky height, to the cathedral: where Mass was performing to an auditory very like that of Lyons, namely, several old women, a baby, and a very self-possessed dog, who had marked out for himself a little course or platform for exercise, beginning at the altar-rails and ending at the door, up and down which constitutional walk he trotted, during the service, as methodically and calmly, as any old gentleman out of doors. It is a bare old church, and the paintings in the roof are sadly defaced by time and damp weather; but the sun was shining in, splendidly, through the red curtains of the windows, and glittering on the altar furniture; and it looked as bright and cheerful as need be.

Going apart, in this church, to see some painting which was being executed in fresco by a French artist and his pupil, I was led to observe more closely than I might otherwise have done, a great number of votive offerings with which the walls of the different chapels were profusely hung. I will not say decorated, for they were very roughly and comically got up; most likely by poor sign-painters, who eke out their living in that way. They were all little pictures: each representing some sickness or calamity from which the person placing it there, had escaped, through the interposition of his or her patron saint, or of the Madonna; and I may refer to

[30]

them as good specimens of the class generally. They are abundant in Italy.

In a grotesque squareness of outline, and impossibility of perspective, they are not unlike the woodcuts in old books; but they were oil-paintings, and the artist, like the painter of the Primrose family, had not been sparing of his colours. In one, a lady was having a toe amputated – an operation which a saintly personage had sailed into the room, upon a couch, to superintend. In another, a lady was lying in bed, tucked up very tight and prim, and staring with much composure at a tripod, with a slop-basin on it; the usual form of washing-stand, and the only piece of furniture, bedsides the bedstead, in her chamber. One would never have supposed her to be labouring under any complaint, beyond the inconvenience of being miraculously wide awake, if the painter had not hit upon the idea of putting all her family on their knees in one corner, with their legs sticking out behind them on the floor, like boot-trees. Above whom, the Virgin, on a kind of blue divan, promised to restore the patient. In another case, a lady was in the very act of being run over, immediately outside the city walls, by a sort of piano-forte van. But the Madonna was there again. Whether the supernatural appearance had startled the horse (a bay griffin), or whether it was invisible to him, I don't know; but he was

[31]

galloping away, ding dong, without the smallest reverence or compunction. On every picture 'Ex voto' was painted in yellow capitals in the sky.

Though votive offerings were not unknown in Pagan Temples, and are evidently among the many compromises made between the false religion and the true, when the true was in its infancy, I could wish that all the other compromises were as harmless. Gratitude and Devotion are Christian qualities; and a grateful, humble, Christian spirit may dictate the observance.

Hard by the Cathedral stands the ancient Palace of the Popes, of which one portion is now a common jail, and another a noisy barrack: while gloomy suites of state apartments, shut up and deserted, mock their own old state and glory, like the embalmed bodies of kings. But we neither went there, to see state rooms, nor soldiers' quarters, nor a common jail, though we dropped some money into a prisoners' box outside, whilst the prisoners, themselves, looked through the iron bars, high up, and watched us eagerly. We went to see the ruins of the dreadful rooms in which the Inquisition used to sit.

A little, old, swarthy woman, with a pair of flashing black eyes – proof that the world hadn't conjured down the devil within her, though it had had between sixty and seventy years to do it in, –

came out of the Barrack Cabaret, of which she was the keeper, with some large keys in her hands, and marshalled us the way that we should go. How she told us, on the way, that she was a Government Officer (*concierge du palais apostolique*), and had been, for I don't know how many years; and how she had shown these dungeons to princes; and how she was the best of dungeon demonstrators; and how she had resided in the palace from an infant, – had been born there, if I recollect right, – I needn't relate. But such a fierce, little, rapid, sparkling, energetic she-devil I never beheld. She was alight and flaming, all the time. Her action was violent in the extreme. She never spoke, without stopping expressly for the purpose. She stamped her feet, clutched us by the arms, flung herself into attitudes, hammered against walls with her keys, for mere emphasis: how whispered as if the Inquisition were there still: now shrieked as if she were on the rack herself; and had a mysterious, hag-like way with her forefinger, when approaching the remains of some new horror – looking back and walking stealthily, and making horrible grimaces – that might alone have qualified her to walk up and down a sick man's counterpane, to the exclusion of all other figures, through a whole fever.

Passing through the court-yard, among groups of idle solders, we turned off by a gate, which this

[33]

She-Goblin unlocked for our admission, and locked again behind us: and entered a narrow court, rendered narrower by fallen stones and heaps of rubbish; part of it choking up the mouth of a ruined subterranean passage, that once communicated (or is said to have done so) with another castle on the opposite bank of the river. Close to this court-yard is a dungeon – we stood within it, in another minute – in the dismal tower *des oubliettes,* where Rienzi was imprisoned, fastened by an iron chain to the very wall that stands there now, but shut out from the sky which now looks down upon it. A few steps brought us to the Cachots, in which the prisoners of the Inquisition were confined for forty-eight hours after their capture, without food or drink, that their constancy might be shaken, even before they were confronted with their gloomy judges. The day has not got in there yet. They are still small cells, shut in by four unyielding, close, hard walls; still profoundly dark; still massively doored and fastened, as of old.

Goblin, looking back as I have described, went softly on, into a vaulted chamber, now used as a store-room: once the chapel of the Holy Office. The place where the tribunal sat, was plain. The platform might have been removed but yesterday. Conceive the parable of the Good Samaritan having been painted on the wall of one of these Inquisition

[34]

chambers! But it was, and may be traced there yet.

High up in the jealous wall, are niches where the faltering replies of the accused were heard and noted down. Many of them had been brought out of the very cell we had just looked into, so awfully; along the same stone passage. We had trodden in their very footsteps.

I am gazing round me, with the horror that the place inspires, when Goblin clutches me by the wrist, and lays, not her skinny finger, but the handle of a key, upon her lip. She invites me, with a jerk, to follow her. I do so. She leads me out into a room adjoining – a rugged room, with a funnel-shaped, contracting roof, open at the top, to the bright day. I ask her what it is. She folds her arms, leers hideously, and stares. I ask again. She glances round, to see that all the little company are there; sits down upon a mound of stones; throws up her arms, and yells out, like a fiend, 'La Salle de la Question!'

The Chamber of Torture! And the roof was made of that shape to stifle the victim's cries! Oh Goblin, Goblin, let us think of this awhile, in silence. Peace, Goblin! Sit with your arms crossed on your short legs, upon that heap of stones, for only five minutes, and then flame out again.

Minutes! Seconds are not marked upon the Palace clock, when, with her eyes flashing fire,

[35]

Goblin is up, in the middle of the chamber, describing, with her sunburnt arms, a wheel of heavy blows. Thus it ran round! cries Goblin. Mash, mash, mash! An endless routine of heavy hammers. Mash, mash, mash! upon the sufferer's limbs. See the stone trough! says Goblin. For the water torture! Gurgle, swill, bloat, burst, for the Redeemer's honour! Suck the bloody rag, deep down into your unbelieving body, Heretic, at every breath you draw! And when the executioner plucks it out, reeking with the smaller mysteries of God's own Image, know us for His chosen servants, true believers in the Sermon on the Mount, elect disciples of Him who never did a miracle but to heal: who never struck a man with palsy, blindness, deafness, dumbness, madness, any one affliction of mankind; and never stretched His blessed hand out, but to give relief and ease!

See! cries Goblin. There the furnace was. There they made the irons red-hot. Those holes supported the sharp stake, on which the tortured persons hung poised: dangling with their whole weight from the roof. 'But;' and Goblin whispers this; 'Monsieur has heard of this tower? Yes? Let Monsieur look down, then!'

A cold air, laden with an earthy smell, falls upon the face of Monsieur; for she has opened, while speaking, a trap-door in the wall. Monsieur looks

[36]

in. Downward to the bottom, upward to the top, of a steep, dark, lofty tower; very dismal, very dark, very cold. The Executioner of the Inquisition, says Goblin, edging in her head to look down also, flung those who were past all further torturing, down here. 'But look! does Monsieur see the black stains on the wall?' A glance, over his shoulder, at Goblin's keen eye, shows Monsieur – and would without the aid of the directing-key – where they are. 'What are they?' 'Blood!'

In October, 1791, when the Revolution was at its height here, sixty persons: men and women ('and priests,' says Goblin, 'priests'): were murdered, and hurled, the dying and the dead, into this dreadful pit, where a quantity of quick-lime was tumbled down upon their bodies. Those ghastly tokens of the massacre were soon no more; but while one stone of the strong building in which the deed was done, remains upon another, there they will lie in the memories of men, as plain to see as the splashing of their blood upon the wall is now.

Was it a portion of the great scheme of Retribution, that the cruel deed should be committed in this place! That a part of the atrocities and monstrous institutions, which had been, for scores of years, at work, to change men's nature, should in its last service, tempt them with the ready means of gratifying their furious and beastly rage! Should

[37]

enable them to show themselves, in the height of
their frenzy, no worse than a great, solemn, legal
establishment, in the height of its power! No worse!
Much better. They used the Tower of the Forgotten, in the name of Liberty – their liberty; an
earth-born creature, nursed in the black mud of the
Bastille moats and dungeons, and necessarily bet-
raying many evidences of its unwholesome
bringing-up – but the Inquisition used it in the
name of Heaven.

Goblin's finger is lifted; and she steals out again,
into the Chapel of the Holy Office. She stops at a
certain part of the flooring. Her great effect is at
hand. She waits for the rest. She darts at the brave
Courier, who is explaining something; hits him a
sounding rap on the hat with the largest key; and
bids him be silent. She assembles us all, round a
little trap-door in the floor, as round a grave.

'Voilà!' she darts down at the ring, and flings the
door open with a crash in her goblin energy, though
it is no light weight. 'Voilà les oubliettes! Voilà les
oubliettes! Subterranean! Frightful! Black! Terrible! Deadly! Les oubliettes de l'Inquisition!'

My blood ran cold, as I looked from Goblin,
down into the vaults, where these forgotten creatures, with recollections of the world outside: of
wives, friends, children, brothers: starved to death,
and made the stones ring with their unavailing

[38]

groans. But, the thrill I felt on seeing the accursed wall below, decayed and broken through, and the sun shining in through its gaping wounds, was like a sense of victory and triumph. I felt exalted with the proud delight of living in these degenerate times, to see it. As if I were the hero of some high achievement! The light in the doleful vaults was typical of the light that has streamed in, on all persecution in God's name, but which is not yet at its noon! It cannot look more lovely to a blind man newly restored to sight, than to a traveller who sees it, calmly and majestically, treading down the darkness of that Infernal Well.

AVIGNON TO GENOA

Goblin, having shown *les oubliettes*, felt that her great *coup* was struck. She let the door fall with a crash, and stood upon it with her arms a-kimbo, sniffing prodigiously.

When we left the place, I accompanied her into her house, under the outer gateway of the fortress, to buy a little history of the building. Her cabaret, a dark, low room, lighted by small windows, sunk in the thick wall – in the softened light, and with its forge-like chimney; its little counter by the door, with bottles, jars and glasses on it; its household implements and scraps of dress against the wall; and a sober-looking woman (she must have a congenial

[39]

life of it, with Goblin) knitting at the door – looked
exactly like a picture by Ostade.

I walked round the building on the outside, in a
sort of dream, and yet with the delightful sense of
having awakened from it, of which the light, down
in the vaults, had given me the assurance. The
immense thickness and giddy height of the walls,
the enormous strength of the massive towers, the
great extent of the building, its gigantic proportions, frowning aspect, and barbarous irregularity,
awaken awe and wonder. The recollection of its
opposite old uses: an impregnable fortress, a luxu-
rious palace, a horrible prison, a place of torture,
the court of the Inquisition: at one and the same
time, a house of feasting, fighting, religion, and
blood: gives to every stone in its huge form a fearful
interest, and imparts new meaning to its incon-
gruities. I could think of little, however, then, or
long afterwards, but the sun in the dungeons. The
palace coming down to be the lounging-place of
noisy soldiers, and being forced to echo their rough
talk, and common oaths, and to have their garments
fluttering from its dirty windows, was some reduc-
tion of its state, and something to rejoice at; but the
day in its cells, and the sky for the roof of its
chambers of cruelty – that was its desolation and
defeat! If I had seen it in a blaze from ditch to
rampart, I should have felt that not that light, nor

all the light in all the fire that burns, could waste it, like the sunbeams in its secret council-chamber, and its prisons.

Before I quit this Palace of the Popes, let me translate from the little history I mentioned just now, a short anecdote, quite appropriate to itself, connected with its adventures.

'An ancient tradition relates, that in 1441, a nephew of Pierre de Lude, the Pope's legate, seriously insulted some distinguished ladies of Avignon, whose relations, in revenge, seized the young man, and horribly mutilated him. For several years the legate kept *his* revenge within his own breast, but he was not the less resolved upon its gratification at last. He even made, in the fulness of time, advances towards a complete reconciliation; and when their apparent sincerity had prevailed, he invited to a splendid banquet, in this palace, certain families, whole families, whom he sought to exterminate. The utmost gaiety animated the repast; but the measures of the legate were well taken. When the dessert was on the board, a Swiss presented himself, with the announcement that a strange ambassador solicited an extraordinary audience. The legate, excusing himself for the moment, to his guests, retired, followed by his officers. Within a few minutes afterwards, five hundred persons were reduced to ashes: the whole of that wing of the

[41]

building having been blown into the air with a terrible explosion!'

After seeing the churches (I will not trouble you with churches just now), we left Avignon that afternoon. The heat being very great, the roads outside the walls were strewn with people fast asleep in every little slip of shade, and with lazy groups, half asleep and half awake, who were waiting until the sun should be low enough to admit of their playing bowls among the burnt-up trees, and on the dusty road. The harvest here was already gathered in, and mules and horses were treading out the corn in the fields. We came, at dusk, upon a wild and hilly country, once famous for brigands; and travelled slowly up a steep ascent. So we went on, until eleven at night, when we halted at the town of Aix (within two stages of Marseilles) to sleep.

The hotel, with all the blinds and shutters closed to keep the light and heat out, was comfortable and airy next morning, and the town was very clean; but so hot, and so intensely light, that when I walked out at noon it was like coming suddenly from the darkened room into crisp blue fire. The air was so very clear, that distant hills and rocky points appeared within an hour's walk; while the town immediately at hand – with a kind of blue wind between me and it – seemed to be white hot, and to

[42]

be throwing off a fiery air from the surface.

We left this town towards evening, and took the road to Marseilles. A dusty road it was; the houses shut up close; and the vines powdered white. At nearly all the cottage doors, women were peeling and slicing onions into earthen bowls for supper. So they had been doing last night all the way from Avignon. We passed one or two shady dark châteaux, surrounded by trees, and embellished with cool basins of water: which were the more refreshing to behold, from the great scarcity of such residences on the road we had travelled. As we approached Marseilles, the road began to be covered with holiday people. Outside the public-houses were parties smoking, drinking, playing draughts and cards, and (once) dancing. But dust, dust, dust, everywhere. We went on, through a long, straggling, dirty suburb, thronged with people; having on our left a dreary slope of land, on which the country-houses of the Marseilles merchants, always staring white, are jumbled and heaped without the slightest order: backs, fronts, sides, and gables towards all points of the compass; until, at last, we entered the town.

I was there, twice or thrice afterwards, in fair weather and foul: and I am afraid there is no doubt that it is a dirty and disagreeable place. But the prospect from the fortified heights, of the beautiful

[43]

Mediterranean, with its lovely rocks and islands, is most delightful. These heights are a desirable retreat, for less picturesque reasons – as an escape from a compound of vile smells perpetually arising from a great harbour full of stagnant water, and befouled by the refuse of innumerable ships with all sorts of cargoes: which, in hot weather, is dreadful in the last degree.

There were foreign sailors, of all nations, in the streets; with red shirts, blue shirts, buff shirts, tawny shirts, and shirts of orange colour; with red caps, blue caps, green caps, great beards, and no beards; in Turkish turbans, glazed English hats, and Neapolitan head-dresses. There were the townspeople sitting in clusters on the pavement, or airing themselves on the tops of their houses, or walking up and down the closest and least airy of Boulevards; and there were crowds of fierce-looking people of the lower sort, blocking up the way, constantly. In the very heart of all this stir and uproar, was the common madhouse; a low, contracted, miserable building, looking straight upon the street, without the smallest screen or court-yard; where chattering mad-men and mad-women were peeping out, through rusty bars, at the staring faces below, while the sun, darting fiercely aslant into their little cells, seemed to dry up their brains, and worry them, as if they were baited by a pack of dogs.

[44]

We were pretty well accommodated at the Hôtel du Paradis, situated in a narrow street of very high houses, with a hairdresser's shop opposite, exhibiting in one of its windows two full-length waxen ladies, twirling round and round: which so enchanted the hairdresser himself, that he and his family sat in arm-chairs, and in cool undresses, on the pavement outside, enjoying the gratification of the passers-by, with lazy dignity. The family had retired to rest when we went to bed, at midnight; but the hairdresser (a corpulent man, in drab slippers) was still sitting there, with his legs stretched out before him, and evidently couldn't bear to have the shutters put up.

Next day we went down to the harbour, where the sailors of all nations were discharging and taking in cargoes of all kinds: fruits, wines, oils, silks, stuffs, velvets, and every manner of merchandise. Taking one of a great number of lively little boats with gay-striped awnings, we rowed away, under the sterns of great ships, under tow-ropes and cables, against and among other boats, and very much too near the sides of vessels that were faint with oranges, to the *Marie Antoinette*, a handsome steamer bound for Genoa, lying near the mouth of the harbour. By-and-by, the carriage, that unwieldy 'trifle from the Pantechnicon,' on a flag barge, bumping against everything, and giving occasion

[45]

for a prodigious quantity of oaths and grimaces, came stupidly alongside; and by five o'clock we were steaming out in the open sea. The vessel was beautifully clean; the meals were served under an awning on deck; the night was calm and clear; the quiet beauty of the sea and sky unspeakable.

THE CALAIS NIGHT MAIL

(from The Uncommercial Traveller)

*'A stout wooden wedge driven in at my right temple
and out at my left, a floating deposit of lukewarm oil
in my throat, and a compression of the bridge of my
nose in a blunt pair of pincers, – these are the personal
sensations by which I know we are off, and by which I
shall continue to know it until I am on the soil of
France.'*

It is an unsettled question with me whether I shall
leave Calais something handsome in my will, or
whether I shall leave it my malediction. I hate it so
much, and yet I am always so very glad to see it,
that I am in a state of constant indecision on this
subject. When I first made acquaintance with
Calais, it was as a maundering young wretch in a
clammy perspiration and dripping saline particles,
who was conscious of no extremities but the one
great extremity, sea-sickness – who was a mere
bilious torso, with a mislaid headache somewhere in
its stomach – who had been put into a horrible
swing in Dover Harbour, and had tumbled giddily
out of it on the French coast, or the Isle of Man, or
anywhere. Times have changed, and now I enter
Calais self-reliant and rational. I know where it is
beforehand, I keep a look out for it, I recognise its

[47]

landmarks when I see any of them, I am acquainted with its ways, and I know – and I can bear – its worst behaviour.

Malignant Calais! Low-lying alligator, evading the eyesight and discouraging hope! Dodging flat streak, now on this bow, now on that, now anywhere, now everywhere, now nowhere! In vain Cape Grinez, coming frankly forth into the sea, exhorts the failing to be stout of heart and stomach: sneaking Calais, prone behind its bar, invites emetically to despair. Even when it can no longer quite conceal itself in its muddy dock, it has an evil way of falling off, has Calais, which is more hopeless than its invisibility. The pier is all but on the bowsprit, and you think you are there – roll, roar, wash! – Calais has retired miles inland, and Dover has burst out to look for it. It has a last dip and slide in its character, has Calais, to be especially commended to the infernal gods. Thrice accursed be that garrison-town, when it dives under the boat's keel, and comes up a league or two to the right, with the packet shivering and spluttering and staring about for it!

Not but what I have my animosities towards Dover. I particularly detest Dover for the self-complacency with which it goes to bed. It always goes to bed (when I am going to Calais) with a more brilliant display of lamp and candle than any other

[48]

town. Mr. and Mrs. Birmingham, host and hostess of the Lord Warden Hotel, are my much esteemed friends, but they are too conceited about the comforts of that establishment when the Night Mail is starting. I know it is a good house to stay at, and I don't want the fact insisted upon in all its warm bright windows at such an hour. I know the Warden is a stationary edifice that never rolls or pitches, and I object to its big outline seeming to insist upon that circumstance, and, as it were, to come over me with it, when I am reeling on the deck of the boat. Beshrew the Warden likewise for obstructing that corner and making the wind so angry as it rushes round. Shall I not know that it blows quite soon enough, without the officious Warden's interference?

As I wait here on board the night packet, for the South-Eastern Train to come down with the Mail, Dover appears to me to be illuminated for some intensely aggravating festivity in my personal dishonour. All its noises smack of taunting praises of the land, and dispraises of the gloomy sea, and of me for going on it. The drums upon the heights have gone to bed, or I know they would rattle taunts against me for having my unsteady footing on this slippery deck. The many gas eyes of the Marine Parade twinkle in an offensive manner, as if with derision. The distant dogs of Dover bark at me in

[49]

my mis-shapen wrappers, as if I were Richard the Third.

A screech, a bell, and two red eyes come gliding down the Admiralty Pier with a smoothness of motion rendered more smooth by the heaving of the boat. The sea makes noises against the pier, as if several hippopotami were lapping at it, and were prevented by circumstances over which they had no control from drinking peaceably. We, the boat, become violently agitated – rumble, hum, scream, roar, and establish an immense family washing-day at each paddle-box. Bright patches break out in the train as the doors of the post-office vans are opened, and instantly stooping figures with sacks upon their backs begin to be beheld among the piles, descending as it would seem in ghostly procession to Davy Jones's Locker. The passengers come on board; a few shadowy Frenchmen, with hatboxes shaped like the stoppers of gigantic case-bottles; a few shadowy Germans in immense fur coats and boots; a few shadowy Englishmen prepared for the worst and pretending not to expect it. I cannot disguise from my uncommercial mind the miserable fact that we are a body of outcasts; that the attendants on us are as scant in number as may serve to get rid of us with the least possible delay; that there are no night-loungers interested in us; that the unwilling lamps shiver and shudder at us; that the sole object

[50]

is to commit us to the deep and abandon us. Lo, the two red eyes glaring in increasing distance, and then the very train itself has gone to bed before we are off!

What is the moral support derived by some sea-going amateurs from an umbrella? Why do certain voyagers across the Channel always put up that article, and hold it up with a grim and fierce tenacity? A fellow-creature near me – whom I only know to *be* a fellow-creature, because of his umbrella: without which he might be a dark bit of cliff, pier, or bulkhead – clutches that instrument with a desperate grasp, that will not relax until he lands at Calais. Is there any analogy, in certain constitutions, between keeping an umbrella up, and keeping the spirits up? A hawser thrown on board with a flop replies 'Stand by!' 'Stand by, below!' 'Half a turn a head!' 'Half a turn a head!' 'Half speed!' 'Half speed!' 'Port!' 'Port!' 'Steady!' 'Steady!' 'Go on!' 'Go on!'

A stout wooden wedge driven in at my right temple and out at my left, a floating deposit of lukewarm oil in my throat, and a compression of the bridge of my nose in a blunt pair of pincers, – these are the personal sensations by which I know we are off, and by which I shall continue to know it until I am on the soil of France. My symptoms have scarcely established themselves comfortably, when

[51]

two or three skating shadows that have been trying
to walk or stand, get flung together, and other two
or three shadows in tarpaulin slide with them into
corners and cover them up. Then the South Fore-
land lights begin to hiccup at us in a way that bodes
no good.

It is at about this period that my detestation of
Calais knows no bounds. Inwardly I resolve afresh
that I never will forgive that hated town. I have
done so before, many times, but that is past. Let me
register a vow. Implacable animosity to Calais
everm—that was an awkward sea, and the funnel
seems of my opinion, for it gives a complaining
roar.

The wind blows stiffly from the Nor'East, the sea
runs high, we ship a deal of water, the night is dark
and cold, and the shapeless passengers lie about in
melancholy bundles, as if they were sorted out for
the laundress; but for my own uncommercial part I
cannot pretend that I am much inconvenienced by
any of these things. A general howling, whistling
flopping gurgling and scooping, I am aware of, and
a general knocking about of Nature; but the impressions I receive are very vague. In a sweet faint
temper, something like the smell of damaged
oranges, I think I should feel languidly benevolent
if I had time. I have not time, because I am under a
curious compulsion to occupy myself with the Irish

melodies. 'Rich and rare were the gems she wore,' is the particular melody to which I find myself devoted. I sing it to myself in the most charming manner and with the greatest expression. Now and then, I raise my head (I am sitting on the hardest of wet seats, in the most uncomfortable of wet attitudes, but I don't mind it,) and notice that I am a whirling shuttlecock between a fiery battledore of a lighthouse on the French coast and a fiery battledore of a lighthouse on the English coast; but I don't notice it particularly, except to feel envenomed in my hatred of Calais. Then I go on again, 'Rich and rare were the ge-ems she-e-e-e wore, And a bright gold ring on her wa-and she bo-ore, But O her beauty was fa-a-a-a-r beyond – I am particularly proud of my execution here, when I become aware of another awkward shock from the sea, and another protest from the funnel, and a fellow-creature at the paddle-box more audibly indisposed than I think he need be – 'Her sparkling gems or snow-white wand, But O her beauty was fa-a-a-a-r beyond' – another awkward one here, and the fellow-creature with the umbrella down and picked up – 'Her spa-a-rkling ge-ems, or her Port! port! steady! steady! snow-white fellow-creature at the paddle-box very selfishly audible, bump roar wash white wand.'

As my execution of the Irish melodies partakes of

[53]

my imperfect perceptions of what is going on
around me, so what is going on around me becomes
something else than what it is. The stokers open the
furnace doors below, to feed the fires, and I am
again on the box of the old Exeter Telegraph fast
coach, and that is the light of the for ever exting-
uished coach-lamps, and the gleam on the hatches
and paddle-boxes is *their* gleam on cottages and
haystacks, and the monotonous noise of the engines
is the steady jingle of the splendid team. Anon, the
intermittent funnel roar of protest at every violent
roll, becomes the regular blast of a high pressure
engine, and I recognise the exceedingly explosive
steamer in which I ascended the Mississippi when
the American civil war was not, and when only its
causes were. A fragment of mast on which the light
of a lantern falls, an end of rope, and a jerking block
or so, become suggestive of Franconi's Circus at
Paris where I shall be this very night mayhap (for it
must be morning now), and they dance to the
self-same time and tune as the trained steed, Black
Raven. What may be the speciality of these waves as
they come rushing on, I cannot desert the pressing
demands made upon me by the gems she wore, to
inquire, but they are charged with something about
Robinson Crusoe, and I think it was in Yarmouth
Roads that he first went a seafaring and was near
foundering (what a terrific sound that word had for

[54]

me when I was a boy!) in his first gale of wind. Still, through all this, I must ask her (who *was* she, I wonder!) for the fiftieth time, and without ever stopping, Does she not fear to stray, So lone and lovely through this bleak way, And are Erin's sons so good or so cold, As not to be tempted by more fellow-creatures at the paddle-box or gold? Sir Knight I feel not the least alarm, No son of Erin will offer me harm, For though they love fellow-creature with umbrella down again and golden store, Sir Knight they what a tremendous one love honour and virtue more: For though they love Stewards with a bull's eye bright, they'll trouble you for your ticket, sir – rough passage to-night!

I freely admit it to be a miserable piece of human weakness and inconsistency, but I no sooner become concsious of those last words from the steward than I being to soften towards Calais. Whereas I have been vindictively wishing that those Calais burghers who came out of their town by a short cut into the History of England, with those fatal ropes round their necks by which they have since been towed into so many cartoons, had all been hanged on the spot, I now begin to regard them as highly respectable and virtuous tradesmen. Looking about me, I see the light of Cape Grinez well astern of the boat on the davits to leeward, and the light of Calais Harbour undeniably at its old tricks, but still ahead and shining. Sentiments of forgiveness of Calais, not to say of attachment to Calais, begin to expand my bosom. I have weak notions that I will stay there a day or two on my way back. A faded and recumbent stranger pausing in a profound reverie over the rim of a basin, asked me what kind of place Calais is? I tell him (Heaven forgive me!) a very agreeable place indeed – rather hilly than otherwise.

So strangely goes the time, and on the whole so quickly – though still I seem to have been on board a week – that I am bumped rolled gurgled washed and pitched into Calais Harbour before her maiden smile has finally lighted her through the Green Isle, When blest for ever is she who relied, On entering Calais at the top of the tide. For we have not to land to-night down among those slimy timbers – covered with green hair as if it were the mermaids' favourite combing place – where one crawls to the surface of the jetty, like a stranded shrimp, but we go steaming up the harbour to the Railway Station Quay. And as we go, the sea washes in and out among piles and planks, with dead heavy beats and in quite a furious manner (whereof we are proud), and the lamps shake in the wind, and the bells of Calais striking One seem to send their vibrations struggling against troubled air, as we have come struggling against troubled water. And now, in the sudden relief and wiping of faces, everybody on

board seems to have had a prodigious double-tooth
out, and to be this very instant free of the Dentist's
hands. And now we all know for the first time how
wet and cold we are, and how salt we are; and now I
love Calais with my heart of hearts!

'Hôtel Dessin!' (but in this case not a vocal cry; it
is but a bright lustre in the eyes of the cheery
representative of that best of inns). 'Hôtel Meurice!'
'Hôtel de France!' 'Hôtel de Calais!' 'The Royal
Hôtel, Sir, Angaishe ouse!' 'You going to Parry,
Sir!' 'Your baggage, registair froo, Sir?' 'Bless ye,
my Touters, bless ye, my commissionaires, bless
ye, my hungry-eyed mysteries in caps of a military
form, who are always here, day or night, fair
weather or foul, seeking inscrutable jobs which I
never see you get! Bless ye, my Custom House
officers in green and grey; permit me to grasp the
welcome hands that descend into my travelling-bag,
one on each side, and meet at the bottom to give my
change of linen a peculiar shake up, as if it were a
measure of chaff or grain! I have nothing to declare,
Monsieur le Douanier, except that when I cease to
breathe, Calais will be found written on my heart.
No article liable to local duty have I with me,
Monsieur l'Officier de l'Octroi, unless the overflow-
ing of a breast devoted to your charming town
should be in that wise chargeable. Ah! see at the
gangway by the twinkling lantern, my dearest

[57]

brother and friend, he once of the Passport Office, he who collects the names! May he be for ever changeless in his buttoned black surtout, with his note-book in his hand, and his tall black hat surmounting his round smiling patient face! Let us embrace, my dearest brother. I am yours à tout jamais – for the whole of ever.

Calais up and doing at the railway station, and Calais down and dreaming in its bed; Calais with something of 'an ancient and fish-like smell' about it, and Calais blown and sea-washed pure; Calais represented at the Buffet by savoury roast fowls, hot coffee, cognac, and Bordeaux; and Calais represented everywhere by flitting persons with a monomania for changing money – though I never shall be able to understand in my present state of existence how they live by it, but I suppose I should, if I understood the currency question – Calais *en gros*, and Calais *en détail*, forgive one who has deeply wronged you. – I was not fully aware of it on the other side, but I meant Dover.

Ding, ding! To the carriages, gentlemen the travellers. Ascend then, gentlemen the travellers from Hazebroucke, Lille, Douai, Bruxelles, Arras, Amiens, and Paris! I, humble representative of the uncommercial interest, ascend with the rest. The train is light to-night, and I share my compartment with but two fellow-travellers; one, a compatriot in

an obsolete cravat, who thinks it is a quite un-
accountable thing that they don't keep 'London
time' on a French railway, and who is made angry
by my modestly suggesting the possibility of Paris
time being more in their way; the other, a young
priest, with a very small bird in a very small cage,
who feeds the small bird with a quill, and then puts
him up in the network above his head, where he
advances twittering, to his front wires, and seems to
address me in an electioneering manner. The compatriot (who crossed in the boat and whom I judge
to be some person of distinction, as he was shut up,
like a stately species of rabbit, in a private hutch on
deck) and the young priest (who joined us at Calais)
are soon asleep, and then the bird and I have it all to
ourselves.

A stormy night; a night that sweeps in the wires
of the electric telegraph with a wild and fitful hand;
a night so very stormy, with the added storm of the
train-progress through it, that when the Guard
comes clambering round to mark the tickets while
we are at full speed (a really horrible performance in
an express train, though he holds on to the open
window by his elbows in the most deliberate manner), he stands in such a whirlwind that I grip him
fast by the collar, and feel it next to manslaughter to
let him go. Still, when he is gone, the small small
bird remains at his front wires feebly twittering to

me – twittering and twittering, until leaning back in my place and looking at him in drowsy fascination, I find that he seems to jog my memory as we rush along.

Uncommercial travellers (thus the small small bird) have lain in their idle thriftless way through all this range of swamp and dyke, as through many other odd places; and about here, as you very well know, are the queer old stone farmhouses, approached by drawbridges, and the windmills that you get at by boats. Here, are the lands where the women hoe and dig, paddling canoe-wise from field to field, and here are the cabarets and other peasant-houses where the stone dove-cotes in the littered yards are as strong as warders' towers in old castles. Here, are the long monotonous miles of canal, with the great Dutch-built barges garishly painted and the towing girls, sometimes harnessed by the fore-head, sometimes by the girdle and the shoulders, not a pleasant sight to see. Scattered through this country are mighty works of Vauban, whom you know about, and regiments of such corporals as you heard of once upon a time, and many a blue-eyed Bebelle. Through these flat districts, in the shining summer days, walk those long grotesque files of young novices in enormous shovel-hats, whom you remember blackening the ground checkered by the avenues of leafy trees. And now that Hazebroucke

[60]

slumbers certain kilometres ahead, recall the summer evening when your dusty feet strolling up from the station tended hap-hazard to a Fair there, where the oldest inhabitants were circling round and round a barrel-organ on hobby-horses, with the greatest gravity, and where the principal show in the Fair was a Religious Richardson's – literally, on its own announcement in great letters, THEATRE RELIGIEUX. In which improving Temple, the dramatic representation was of 'all the interesting events in the life of our Lord, from the Manger to the Tomb;' the principal female character, without any reservation or exception, being at the moment of your arrival, engaged in trimming the external Moderators (as it was growing dusk), while the next principal female character took the money, and the Young Saint John disported himself upside down on the platform.

Looking up at this point to confirm the small small bird in every particular he has mentioned, I find he has ceased to twitter, and has put his head under his wing. Therefore, in my different way I follow the good example.

A Flight

(from Reprinted Pieces)

*'So, I pass to my hotel, enchanted; sup, enchanted; go
to bed, enchanted; pushing back this morning (if it
really were this morning) into the remoteness of time,
blessing the South-Eastern Company for realising the
Arabian Nights in these prose days, murmuring, as I
wing my idle flight into the land of dreams, "No
hurry, ladies and gentlemen, going to Paris in eleven
hours. It is so well done, that there really is no hurry!"'*

When Don Diego de – I forget his name – the
inventor of the last new Flying Machines, price so
many francs for ladies, so many more for gentlemen
– when Don Diego, by permission of Deputy
Chaff-wax and his noble band, shall have taken out
a Patent for the Queen's dominions, and shall have
opened a commodious Warehouse in an airy situation; and when all persons of any gentility will keep
at least a pair of wings, and be seen skimming about
in every direction; I shall take a flight to Paris (as I
soar round the world) in a cheap and independent
manner. At present, my reliance is on the South-
Eastern Railway Company, in whose Express Train
here I sit, at eight of the clock on a very hot
morning, under the very hot roof of the Terminus
at London Bridge, in danger of being 'forced' like a
cucumber or a melon, or a pine-apple. And talking

of pine-apples, I suppose there never were as many pine-apples in a Train as there appear to be in this Train.

Whew! The hot-house air is faint with pine-apples. Every French citizen or citizeness is carrying pine-apples home. The compact little Enchantress in the corner of my carriage (French actress, to whom I yielded up my heart under the auspices of that brave child, 'Meat-chell,' at the St. James's Theatre the night before last) has a pine-apple in her lap. Compact Enchantress's friend, confidante, mother, mystery, Heaven knows what, has two pine-apples in her lap, and a bundle of them under the seat. Tobacco-smoky Frenchman in Algerine wrapper with peaked hood behind, who might be Abd-el-Kader dyed rifle-green, and who seems to be dressed entirely in dirt and braid, carries pine-apples in a covered basket. Tall, grave, melancholy Frenchman, with black Vandyke beard, and hair close-cropped, with expansive chest to waistcoast, and compressive waist to coat: saturnine as to his pantaloons, calms as to his feminine boots, precious as to his jewellery, smooth and white as to his linene: dark-eyed, high-foreheaded, hawk-nosed – got up, one thinks, like Lucifer or Mephistopheles, or Zamiel, transformed into a highly genteel Parisian – has the green end of a pine-apple sticking out of his neat valise.

Whew! If I were to be kept here long, under this forcing-frame, I wonder what would become of me – whether I should be forced into a giant, or should sprout or blow into some other phenomenon! Compact Enchantress is not ruffled by the heat – she is always composed, always compact. O look at her little ribbons, frills and edges, at her shawl, at her gloves, at her hair, at her bracelets, at her bonnet, at everything about her! How is it accomplished? What does she do to be so neat? How is it that every trifle she wears belongs to her, and cannot choose but be a part of her? And even Mystery, look at *her*! A model. Mystery is not young, not pretty, though still of an average candlelight passability; but she does such miracles in her own behalf, that, one of these days, when she dies, they'll be amazed to find an old woman in her bed, distantly like her. She was an actress once, I shouldn't wonder, and had a Mystery attendant on herself. Perhaps, Compact Enchantress will live to be a Mystery, and to wait with a shawl at the side-scenes, and to sit opposite Mademoiselle in railway carriages, and smile and talk subserviently, as Mystery does now. That's hard to believe!

Two Englishmen, and now our carriage is full. First Englishman, in the monied interest – flushed, highly respectable – Stock Exchange, perhaps – City, certainly. Faculties of second Englishman

[64]

entirely absorbed in hurry. Plunges into the carriage, blind. Calls out of window concerning his luggage, deaf. Suffocates himself under pillows of great-coats, for no reason, and in a demented manner. Will receive no assurance from any porter whatsoever. Is stout and hot, and wipes his head, and makes himself hotter by breathing so hard. Is totally incredulous respecting assurance of Collected Guard, that 'there's no hurry.' No hurry! And a flight to Paris in eleven hours!

It is all one to me in this drowsy corner, hurry or no hurry. Until Don Diego shall send home my wings, my flight is with the South-Eastern Company. I can fly with the South-Eastern more lazily, at all events, than in the upper air. I have but to sit here thinking as idly as I please, and be whisked away. I am not accountable to anybody for the idleness of my thoughts in such an idle summer flight; my flight is provided for by the South-Eastern and is no business of mine.

The bell! With all my heart. It does not require *me* to do so much as even to flap my wings. Something snorts for me, something shrieks for me, something proclaims to everything else that it had better keep out of my way, – and away I go.

Ah! The fresh air is pleasant after the forcing-frame, though it does blow over these interminable streets, and scatter the smoke of this vast wilderness of chimneys. Here we are – no, I mean there we were, for it has darted far into the rear – in Bermondsey where the tanners live. Flash! The distant shipping in the Thames is gone. Whirr! The little streets of new brick and red tile, with here and there a flagstaff growing like a wall weed out of the scarlet beans, and everywhere, plenty of open sewer and ditch for the promotion of the public health, have been fired off in a volley. Whizz! Dust-heaps, market-gardens, and waste grounds. Rattle! New Cross Station. Shock! There we were at Croydon. Bur-r-r-r! The tunnel.

I wonder why it is that when I shut my eyes in a tunnel I begin to feel as if I were going at an Express pace the other way. I am clearly going back to London now. Compact Enchantress must have forgotten something, and reversed the engine. No! After long darkness, pale fitful streaks of light appear. I am still flying on for Folkestone. The streaks grow stronger – become continuous – become the ghost of day – become the living day – became I mean – the tunnel is miles and miles away, and here I fly through sunlight, all among the harvest and the Kentish hops.

There is a dreamy pleasure in this flying. I wonder where it was, and when it was, that we exploded, blew into space somehow, a Parliamentary Train, with a crowd of heads and faces looking

[66]

at us out of cages, and some hats waving. Monied Interest says it was at Reigate Station. Expounds to Mystery how Reigate Station is so many miles from London, which Mystery again develops to Compact Enchantress. There might be neither a Reigate nor a London for me, as I fly away among the Kentish hops and harvest. What do *I* care?

Bang! We have let another Station off, and fly away regardless. Everything is flying. The hop-gardens turn gracefully towards me, presenting regular avenues of hops in rapid flight, then whirl away. So do the pools and rushes, haystacks, sheep, clover in full bloom delicious to the sight and smell, corn-sheaves, cherry-orchards, apple-orchards, reapers, gleaners, hedges, gates, fields that taper off into little angular corners, cottages, gardens, now and then a church. Bang, bang! A double-barrelled Station! Now a wood, now a bridge, now a landscape, now a cutting, now a – Bang! a single-barrelled Station – there was a cricket-match somewhere with two white tents, and then four flying cows, then turnips – now the wires of the electric telegraph are all alive, and spin, and blur their edges, and go up and down, and make the intervals between each other most irregular: contracting and expanding in the strangest manner. Now we slacken. With a screwing, and a grinding, and a smell of water thrown on ashes, now we stop!

[67]

Demented Traveller, who has been for two or three minutes watchful, clutches his great-coats, plunges at the door, rattles it, cries 'Hi!' eager to embark on board of impossible packets, far inland. Collected Guard appears. 'Are you for Tunbridge, sir?' 'Tunbridge? No. Paris.' 'Plenty of time, sir. No hurry. Five minutes here, sir, for refreshment.' I am so blest (anticipating Zamiel, by half a second) as to procure a glass of water for Compact Enchantress.

Who would suppose we had been flying at such a rate, and shall take wing again directly? Refreshment-room full, platform full, porter with watering-pot deliberately cooling a hot wheel, another porter with equal deliberation helping the rest of the wheels bountifully to ice cream. Monied Interest and I re-entering the carriage first, and being there alone, he intimates to me that the French are 'no go' as a Nation. I ask why? He says, that Reign of Terror of theirs was quite enough. I venture to inquire whether he remembers anything that preceded said Reign of Terror? He says not particularly. 'Because,' I remark, 'the harvest that is reaped, has sometimes been sown.' Monied Interest repeats, as quite enough for him, that the French are revolutionary, – 'and always at it.'

Bell. Compact Enchantress, helped in by Zamiel (whom the stars confound!), gives us her charming

little side-box look, and smites me to the core.
Mystery eating sponge-cake. Pine-apple atmos-
phere faintly tinged with suspicions of sherry.
Demented Traveller flits past the carriage, looking
for it. Is blind with agitation, and can't see it. Seems
singled out by Destiny to be the only unhappy
creature in the flight, who has any cause to hurry
himself. Is nearly left behind. Is seized by Collected
Guard after the Train is in motion, and bundled in.
Still, has lingering suspicions that there must be a
boat in the neighbourhood, and will look wildly out
of window for it.

Flight resumed. Corn-sheaves, hop-gardens,
reapers, gleaners, apple-orchards, cherry-orchards,
Stations single and double-barrelled, Ashford.
Compact Enchantress (constantly talking to Mystery, in an exquisite manner) gives a little scream; a
sound that seems to come from high up in her
precious little head; from behind her bright little
eyebrows. 'Great Heavens, my pine-apple! My
Angel! It is lost!' Mystery is desolated. A search
made. It is not lost. Zamiel finds it. I curse him
(flying) in the Persian manner. May his face be
turned upside down, and jackasses sit upon his
uncle's grave!

Now fresher air, now glimpses of unenclosed
Down-land with flapping crows flying over it whom
we soon out-fly, now the Sea, now Folkestone at a

quarter after ten. 'Tickets ready, gentlemen!' Demented dashes at the door. 'For Paris, sir?' No hurry.

Not the least. We are dropped slowly down to the
Port, and sidle to and fro (the whole Train) before
the insensible Royal George Hotel, for some ten
minutes. The Royal George takes no more heed of
us than its namesake under water at Spithead, or
under earth at Windsor, does. The Royal George's
dog lies winking and blinking at us, without taking
the trouble to sit up; and the Royal George's
'wedding party' at the open window (who seem, I
must say, rather tired of bliss) don't bestow a
solitary glance upon us, flying thus to Paris in
eleven hours. The first gentleman in Folkestone is
evidently used up, on this subject.

Meanwhile, Demented chafes. Conceives that
every man's hand is against him, and exerting itself
to prevent his getting to Paris. Refuses consolation.
Rattles door. Sees smoke on the horizon, and
'knows' it's the boat gone without him. Monied
Interest resentfully explains that *he* is going to Paris
too. Demented signifies that if Monied Interest
chooses to be left behind, *he* don't.

'Refreshments in the Waiting-Room, ladies and
gentlemen. No hurry, ladies and gentlemen, for
Paris. No hurry whatever!'

Twenty minutes' pause, by Folkestone clock, for
looking at Enchantress while she eats a sandwich,

[70]

and at Mystery while she eats of everything there that is eatable, from pork-pie, sausage, jam, and gooseberries, to lumps of sugar. All this time, there is a very waterfall of luggage, with a spray of dust, tumbling slantwise from the pier into the steamboat. All this time, Demented (who has no business with it) watches it with staring eyes, fiercely requiring to be shown his luggage. When it at last concludes the cataract, he rushes hotly to refresh – is shouted after, pursued, jostled, brought back, pitched into the departing steamer upside down, and caught by mariners disgracefully.

A lovely harvest-day, a cloudless sky, a tranquil sea. The piston-rods of the engines so regularly coming up from below, to look (as well they may) at the bright weather, and so regularly almost knocking their iron heads against the cross beam of the skylight, and never doing it! Another Parisian actress is on board, attended by another Mystery. Compact Enchantress greets her sister artist – Oh, the Compact One's pretty teeth! – and Mystery greets Mystery. *My* Mystery soon ceases to be conversational – is taken poorly, in a word, having lunched too miscellaneously – and goes below. The remaining Mystery then smiles upon the sister artists (who, I am afraid, wouldn't greatly mind stabbing each other), and is upon the whole ravished.

[71]

And now I find that all the French people on board begin to grow, and all the English people to shrink. The French are nearing home, and shaking off a disadvantage, whereas we are shaking it on. Zamiel is the same man, and Abd-el-Kader is the same man, but each seems to come into possession of an indescribable confidence that departs from us – from Monied Interest, for instance, and from me. Just what they gain, we lose. Certain British 'Gents' about the steersman, intellectually nurtured at home on parody of everything and truth of nothing, become subdued, and in a manner forlorn; and when the steersman tells them (not exultingly) how he has 'been upon this station now eight year, and never see the old town of Bullum yet,' one of them, with an imbecile reliance on a reed, asks him what he considers to be the best hotel in Paris?

Now, I tread upon French ground, and am greeted by the three charming words, Liberty, Equality, Fraternity, painted up (in letters a little too thin for their height) on the Custom-house wall – also by the sight of large cocked hats, without which demonstrative head-gear nothing of a public nature can be done upon this soil. All the rabid Hotel population of Boulogne howl and shriek outside a distant barrier, frantic to get at us. Demented, by some unlucky means peculiar to himself, is delivered over to their fury, and is

[72]

presently seen struggling in a whirlpool of Touters –
is somehow understood to be going to Paris – is,
with infinite noise, rescued by two cocked hats, and
brought into Custom-house bondage with the rest
of us.

Here, I resign the active duties of life to an eager
being, of preternatural sharpness, with a shelving
forehead and a shabby snuff-coloured coat, who
(from the wharf) brought me down with his eye
before the boat came into port. He darts upon my
luggage, on the floor where all the luggage is strewn
like a wreck at the bottom of the great deep; gets it
proclaimed and weighed as the property of 'Monsieur a traveller unknown;' pays certain francs for
it, to a certain functionary behind a Pigeon Hole,
like a pay-box at a Theatre (the arrangements in
general are on a wholesale scale, half military and
half theatrical); and I suppose I shall find it when I
come to Paris – he says I shall. I know nothing
about it, except that I pay him his small fee, and
pocket the ticket he gives me, and sit upon a
counter, involved in the general distraction.

Railway station. 'Lunch or dinner, ladies and
gentlemen. Plenty of time for Paris. Plenty of time!'
Large hall, long counter, long strips of dining-table,
bottles of wine, plates of meat, roast chickens, little
loaves of bread, bains of soup, little caraffes of
brandy, cakes and fruit. Comfortably restored from

[73]

these resources, I begin to fly again.

I saw Zamiel (before I took wing) presented to Compact Enchantress and Sister Artist, by an officer in uniform, with a waist like a wasp's, and pantaloons like two balloons. They all got into the next carriage together, accompanied by the two Mysteries. They laughed. I am alone in the carriage (for I don't consider Demented anybody) and alone in the world.

Fields, windmills, low grounds, pollard-trees, windmills, fields, fortifications, Abbeville, soldiering and drumming. I wonder where England is, and when I was there last – about two years ago, I should say. Flying in and out among these trenches and batteries, skimming the clattering drawbridges, looking down into the stagnant ditches, I become a prisoner of state, escaping. I am confined with a comrade in a fortress. Our room is in an upper story. We have tried to get up the chimney, but there's an iron grating across it, imbedded in the masonry. After months of labour, we have worked the grating loose with the poker, and can lift it up. We have also made a hook, and twisted our rugs and blankets into ropes. Our plan is, to go up the chimney, hook our ropes to the top, descend hand over hand upon the roof of the guard-house far below, shake the hook loose, watch the opportunity of the sentinel's pacing away, hook again, drop into

[74]

the ditch, swim across it, creep into the shelter of the wood. The time is come – a wild and stormy night. We are up the chimney, we are on the guard-house roof, we are swimming in the murky ditch, when lo! 'Qui v'la?' a bugle, the alarm, a crash! What is it? Death? No, Amiens.

More fortifications, more soldiering and drumming, more basins of soup, more little loaves of bread, more bottles of wine, more caraffes of brandy, more time for refreshment. Everything good, and everything ready. Bright, unsubstantial-looking, scenic sort of station. People waiting. Houses, uniforms, beards, moustaches, some sabots, plenty of neat women, and a few old-visaged children. Unless it be a delusion born of my giddy flight, the grown-up people and the children seem to change places in France. In general, the boys and girls are little old men and women, and the men and women lively boys and girls.

Bugle, shriek, flight resumed. Monied Interest has come into my carriage. Says the manner of refreshing is 'not bad,' but considers it French. Admits great dexterity and politeness in the attendants. Thinks a decimal currency may have something to do with their despatch in settling accounts, and don't know but what it's sensible and convenient. Adds, however, as a general protest, that they're a revolutionary people – and always at it.

[75]

Ramparts, canals, cathedral, river, soldiering and drumming, open country, river, earthenware manufactures, Creil. Again ten minutes. Not even Demented in a hurry. Station, a drawing room with a verandah: like a planter's house. Monied Interest considers it a band-box, and not made to last. Little round tables in it, at one of which the Sister Artists and attendant Mysteries are established with Wasp and Zamiel, as if they were going to stay a week.

Anon, with no more trouble than before, I am flying again, and lazily wondering as I fly. What has the South-Eastern done with all the horrible little villages we used to pass through in the *Diligence*? What have they done with all the summer dust, with all the winter mud, with all the dreary avenues of little trees, with all the ramshackle post-yards, with all the beggars (who used to turn out at night with bits of lighted candle, to look in at the coach windows), with all the long-tailed horses who were always biting one another, with all the big post-illions in jack-boots – with all the mouldy cafés that we used to stop at, where a long mildewed table-cloth, set forth with jovial bottles of vinegar and oil, and with a Siamese arrangement of pepper and salt, was never wanting? Where are the grass-grown little towns, the wonderful little market-places all uncon-scious of markets, the shops that nobody kept, the streets that nobody trod, the churches that nobody

[76]

went to, the bells that nobody rang, the tumble-down old buildings plastered with many-coloured bills that nobody read? Where are the two-and-twenty weary hours of long long day and night journey, sure to be either insupportably hot or insupportably cold? Where are the pains in my bones, where are the fidgets in my legs, where is the Frenchman with the nightcap who never *would* have the little coupé-window down, and who always fell upon me when he went to sleep, and always slept all night snoring onions?

A voice breaks in with 'Paris! Here we are!'

I have overflown myself, perhaps, but I can't believe it. I feel as if I were enchanted or bewitched. It is barely eight o'clock yet – it is nothing like half-past – when I have had my luggage examined at that briskest of Custom-houses attached to the station, and am rattling over the pavement in a hackney-cabriolet.

Surely, not the pavement of Paris? Yes, I think it is, too. I don't know any other place where there are all these high houses, all these haggard-looking wine shops, all these billiard tables, all these stocking-makers with flat red or yellow legs of wood for signboard, all these fuel shops with stacks of billets painted outside, and real billets sawing in the gutter, all these dirty corners of streets, all these cabinet pictures over dark doorways representing discreet matrons nursing babies. And yet this morning – I'll think of it in a warm-bath.

Very like a small room that I remember in the Chinese baths upon the Boulevard, certainly; and, though I see it through the steam, I think that I might swear to that peculiar hot-linen basket, like a large wicker hour-glass. When can it have been that I left home? When was it that I paid 'through to Paris' at London Bridge, and discharged myself of all responsibility, except the preservation of a voucher ruled into three divisions, of which the first was snipped off at Folkestone, the second aboard the boat, and the third taken at my journey's end? It seems to have been ages ago. Calculation is useless. I will go out for a walk.

The crowds in the streets, the lights in the shops and balconies, the elegance, variety, and beauty of their decorations, the number of the theatres, the brilliant cafés with their windows thrown up high and their vivacious groups at little tables on the pavement, the light and glitter of the houses turned as it were inside out, soon convince me that it is no dream; that I am in Paris, howsoever I got here. I stroll down to the sparkling Palais Royal, up the Rue de Rivoli, to the Place Vendôme. As I glance into a print-shop window, Monied Interest, my late travelling companion, comes upon me, laughing with the highest relish of disdain. 'Here's a people!'

he says, pointing to Napoleon in the window and Napoleon on the column. 'Only one idea all over Paris! A monomania!' Humph! I THINK I have seen Napoleon's match? There WAS a statue, when I came away, at Hyde Park Corner, and another in the City, and a print or two in the shops.

I walk up to the Barrière de l'Etoile, sufficiently dazed by my flight to have a pleasant doubt of the reality of everything about me; of the lively crowd, the overhanging trees, the performing dogs, the hobby-horses, the beautiful perspectives of shining lamps: the hundred and one enclosures, where the singing is, in gleaming orchestras of azure and gold, and where a star-eyed Houri comes round with a box for voluntary offerings. So, I pass to my hotel, enchanted; sup, enchanted; go to bed, enchanted; pushing back this morning (if it really were this morning) into the remoteness of time, blessing the South-Eastern Company for realising the Arabian Nights in these prose days, murmuring, as I wing my idle flight into the land of dreams, 'No hurry, ladies and gentlemen, going to Paris in eleven hours. It is so well done, that there really is no hurry!'

[79]

OUR FRENCH WATERING-PLACE
(from Reprinted Pieces)

'It is more picturesque and quaint than half the innocent places which tourists, following their leader like sheep, have made impostors of. To say nothing of its houses with grave courtyards, its queer by-corners, and its many-windowed streets white and quiet in the sunlight, there is an ancient belfry in it that would have been in all the Annuals and Albums, going and gone, these hundred years, if it had but been more expensive to get at.' Boulogne, the subject of this essay, became Dickens's favourite resort in the 1850s, and he spent three summers there in 1853–1855. This piece, reflecting in its title the earlier 'Our English Watering-Place' on Broadstairs, appeared in Household Words in 1854.

Having earned by many years of fidelity, the right to be sometimes inconstant to our English watering-place, we have dallied for two or three seasons with a French watering-place: once solely known to us as a town with a very long street, beginning with an abattoir and ending with a steam-boat, which it seemed our fate to behold only at daybreak on winter mornings, when (in the days before continental railroads), just sufficiently awake to know that we were most uncomfortably asleep, it was our destiny always to clatter through it, in the coupé of the diligence from Paris, with a sea of mud behind

[80]

us, and a sea of tumbling waves before. In relation to which latter monster, our mind's eye now recalls a worthy Frenchman in a seal-skin cap with a braided hood over it, once our travelling companion in the coupé aforesaid, who, waking up with a pale and crumpled visage, and looking ruefully out at the grim row of breakers enjoying themselves fanatically on an instrument of torture called 'the Bar,' inquired of us whether we were ever sick at sea? Both to prepare his mind for the abject creature we were presently to become, and also to afford him consolation, we replied, 'Sir, your servant is always sick when it is possible to be so.' He returned, altogether uncheered by the bright example, 'Ah, Heaven, but I am always sick, even when it is *im*possible to be so.'

The means of communication between the French capital and our French watering-place are wholly changed since those days; but the Channel remains unbridged as yet, and the old floundering and knocking about go on there. It must be confessed that saving in reasonable (and therefore rare) sea-weather, the act of arrival at our French watering-place from England is difficult to be achieved with dignity. Several little circumstances combine to render the visitor an object of humiliation. In the first place, the steam no sooner touches the port, than all the passengers fall into captivity:

[81]

being boarded by an overpowering force of Custom-house officers, and marched into a gloomy dungeon. In the second place, the road to this dungeon is fenced off with ropes breast-high, and outside those ropes all the English in the place who have lately been sea-sick and are now well, assemble in their best clothes to enjoy the degradation of their dilapidated fellow-creatures. 'Oh, my gracious! how ill this one has been!' 'Here's a damp one coming next!' '*Here's* a pale one!' 'Oh! Ain't he green in the face, this next one!' Even we ourself (not deficient in natural dignity) have a lively remembrance of staggering up this detested lane one September day in a gale of wind, when we were received like an irresistible comic actor, with a burst of laughter and applause, occasioned by the extreme imbecility of our legs.

We were coming to the third place. In the third place, the captives, being shut up in the gloomy dungeon, are strained, two or three at a time, into an inner cell, to be examined as to passports; and across the doorway of communication stands a military creature making a bar of his arm. Two ideas are generally present to the British mind during these ceremonies; first, that it is necessary to make for the cell with violent struggles, as if it were a life-boat and the dungeon a ship going down; secondly, that the military creature's arm is a national affront, which the government at home ought instantly to 'take up.' The British mind and body becoming heated by these fantasies, delirious answers are made to inquiries, and extravagant actions performed. Thus, Johnson persists in giving Johnson as his baptismal name, and substituting for his ancestral designation the national 'Dam!' Neither can he by any means be brought to recognise the distinction between a portmanteau-key and a passport, but will obstinately persevere in tendering the one when asked for the other. This brings him to the fourth place, in a state of mere idiotcy; and when he is, in the fourth place, cast out at a little door into a howling wilderness of touters, he becomes a lunatic with wild eyes and floating hair until rescued and soothed. If friendless and unrescued, he is generally put into a railway omnibus and taken to Paris.

But our French watering-place, when it is once got into, is a very enjoyable place. It has a varied and beautiful country around it, and many characteristic and agreeable things within it. To be sure, it might have fewer bad smells and less decaying refuse, and it might be better drained, and much cleaner in many parts, and therefore infinitely more healthy. Still, it is a bright, airy, pleasant, cheerful town; and if you were to walk down either of its three well-paved main streets, towards five o'clock

[83]

in the afternoon, when delicate odours of cookery
fill the air, and its hotel windows (it is full of hotels)
give glimpses of long tables set out for dinner, and
made to look sumptuous by the aid of napkins
folded fan-wise, you would rightly judge it to be an
uncommonly good town to eat and drink in.

We have an old walled town, rich in cool public
wells of water, on the top of a hill within and above
the present business-town; and if it were some
hundreds of miles further from England, instead of
being, on a clear day, within sight of the grass
growing in the crevices of the chalk-cliffs of Dover,
you would long ago have been bored to death about
that town. It is more picturesque and quaint than
half the innocent places which tourists, following
their leader like sheep, have made impostors of. To
say nothing of its houses with grave courtyards, its
queer by-corners, and its many-windowed streets
white and quiet in the sunlight, there is an ancient
belfry in it that would have been in all the Annuals
and Albums, going and gone, these hundred years,
if it had but been more expensive to get at. Happily
it has escaped so well, being only in our French
watering-place, that you may like it of your own
accord in a natural manner, without being required
to go into convulsions about it. We regard it as one
of the later blessings of our life, that BILKINS, the
only authority on Taste, never took any notice that

[84]

we can find out, of our French watering-place. Bilkins never wrote about it, never pointed out anything to be seen in it, never measured anything in it, always left it alone. For which relief, Heaven bless the town and the memory of the immortal Bilkins likewise!

There is a charming walk, arched and shaded by trees, on the old walls that form the four sides of this High Town, whence you get glimpses of the streets below, and changing views of the other town and of the river, and of the hills and of the sea. It is made more agreeable and peculiar by some of the solemn houses that are rooted in the deep streets below, bursting into a fresher existence a-top, and having doors and windows, and even gardens, on these ramparts. A child going in at the courtyard gate of one of these houses, climbing up the many stairs, and coming out at the fourth-floor window, might conceive himself another Jack, alighting on enchanted ground from another bean-stalk. It is a place wonderfully populous in children; English children, with governesses reading novels as they walk down the shady lanes of trees, or nursemaids interchanging gossip on the seats; French children with their smiling bonnes in snow-white caps, and themselves – if little boys – in straw head-gear like beehives, work-baskets and church hassocks. Three years ago, there were three weazen old men, one bearing a frayed red ribbon in his threadbare button-hole, always to be found walking together among these children, before dinner-time. If they walked for an appetite, they doubtless lived en pension – were contracted for – otherwise their poverty would have made it a rash action. They were stooping, blear-eyed, dull old men, slip-shod and shabby, in long-skirted short-waisted coats and meagre trousers, and yet with a ghost of gentility hovering in their company. They spoke little to each other, and looked as if they might have been politically discontented if they had had vitality enough. Once, we overheard red-ribbon feebly complain to the other two that somebody, or something, was 'a Robber;' and then they all three set their mouths so that they would have ground their teeth if they had had any. The ensuing winter gathered red-ribbon unto the great company of faded ribbons, and next year the remaining two were there – getting themselves entangled with hoops and dolls – familiar mysteries to the children – probably in the eyes of most of them, harmless creatures who had never been like children, and whom children could never be like. Another winter came, and another old man went, and so, this present year, the last of the triumvirate left off walking – it was no good, now – and sat by himself on a little solitary bench, with the hoops and the dolls as lively as ever all about him.

In the Place d'Armes of this town, a little decayed market is held, which seems to slip through the old gateway, like water, and go rippling down the hill, to mingle with the murmuring market in the lower town, and get lost in its movement and bustle. It is very agreeable on an idle summer morning to pursue this market-stream from the hill-top. It begins, dozingly and dully, with a few sacks of corn; starts into a surprising collection of boots and shoes; goes brawling down the hill in a diversified channel of old cordage, old iron, old crockery, old clothes, civil and military, old rags, new cotton goods, flaming prints of saints, little looking-glasses, and incalculable lengths of tape; dives into a backway, keeping out of sight for a little while, as streams will, or only sparkling for a moment in the shape of a market drinking-shop; and suddenly reappears behind the great church, shooting itself into a bright confusion of white-capped women and blue-bloused men, poultry, vegetables, fruits, flow-ers, pots, pans, praying-chairs, soldiers, country butter, umbrellas and other sun-shades, girl-porters waiting to be hired with baskets at their backs, and one weazen little old man in a cocked hat, wearing a cuirass of drinking-glasses and carrying on his shoulder a crimson temple fluttering with flags, like a glorified pavior's rammer without the handle, who

[87]

rings a little bell in all parts of the scene, and cries his cooling drink Hola, Hola, H-o-o! in a shrill cracked voice that somehow makes itself heard above all the chaffering and vending hum. Early in the afternoon, the whole course of the stream is dry. The praying-chairs are put back in the church, the umbrellas are folded up, the unsold goods are carried away, the stalls and stands disappear, the square is swept, the hackney coaches lounge there to be hired, and on all the country roads (if you walk about, as much as we do) you will see the peasant women, always neatly and comfortably dressed, riding home, with the pleasantest saddle-furniture of clean milk-pails, bright butter-kegs, and the like, on the jolliest little donkeys in the world.

We have another market in our French watering-place – that is to say, a few wooden hutches in the open street, down by the Port – devoted to fish. Our fishing-boats are famous everywhere; and our fishing people, though they love lively colours and taste is neutral (see Bilkins), are among the most picturesque people we ever encountered. They have not only a quarter of their own in the town itself, but they occupy whole villages of their own on the neighbouring cliffs. Their churches and chapels are their own; they consort with one another, they intermarry among themselves, their customs are

[88]

their own, and their costume is their own and never changes. As soon as one of their boys can walk, he is provided with a long bright red nightcap; and one of their men would as soon think of going afloat without his head, as without that indispensable appendage to it. Then, they wear the noblest boots, with the hugest tops – flapping and bulging over anyhow; above which, they encase themselves in such wonderful overalls and petticoat trousers, made to all appearance of tarry old sails, so additionally stiffened with pitch and salt, that the wearers have a walk of their own, and go straddling and swinging about among the boats and barrels and nets and rigging, a sight to see. Then, their younger women, by dint of going down to the sea barefoot, to fling their baskets into the boats as they come in with the tide, and bespeak the first fruits of the haul with propitiatory promises to love and marry that dear fisherman who shall fill that basket like an Angel, have the finest legs ever carved by Nature in the brightest mahogany, and they walk like Juno. Their eyes, too, are so lustrous that their long gold ear-rings turn dull beside those brilliant neighbours; and when they are dressed, what with these beauties, and their fine fresh faces, and their many petticoats, always clean and smart, and never too long – and their home-made stockings, mulberry-coloured, blue, brown, purple, lilac –

[89]

which the older women, taking care of the Dutch-looking children, sit in all sorts of places knitting, knitting, knitting from morning to night – and what with their little saucy bright blue jackets, knitted too, and fitting close to their handsome figures; and what with the natural grace with which they wear the commonest cap, or fold the commonest hand-kerchief round their luxuriant hair – we say, in a word and out of breath, that taking all these premises into our consideration, it has never been a matter of the least surprise to us that we have never once met, in the cornfields, on the dusty roads, by the breezy windmills, on the plots of short sweet grass overhanging the sea – anywhere – a young fisherman and fisherwoman of our French watering-place together, but the arm of that fisher-man has invariably been, as a matter of course and without any absurd attempt to disguise so plain a necessity, round the neck or waist of that fisher-woman. And we have had no doubt whatever, standing looking at their uphill streets, house rising above house, and terrace above terrace, and bright garments here and there lying sunning on rough stone parapets, that the pleasant mist on all such objects, caused by their being seen through the brown nets hung across on poles to dry, is, in the eyes of every true young fisherman, a mist of love and beauty, setting off the goddess of his heart.

[90]

Moreover, it is to be observed that these are an industrious people, and a domestic people, and an honest people. And though we are aware that at the bidding of Bilkins it is our duty to fall down and worship the Neapolitans, we make bold very much to prefer the fishing people of our French watering-place – especially since our last visit to Naples within these twelve months, when we found only four conditions of men remaining in the whole city: to wit, lazzaroni, priests, spies, and soldiers, and all of them beggars; the paternal government having banished all its subjects except the rascals.

But we can never henceforth separate our French watering-place from our own landlord of two summers, M. Loyal Devasseur, citizen and town-councillor. Permit us to have the pleasure of presenting M. Loyal Devasseur.

His own family name is simply Loyal; but as he is married, and as in that part of France a husband always adds to his own name the family name of his wife, he writes himself Loyal Devasseur. He owns a compact little estate of some twenty or thirty acres on a lofty hill-side, and on it he has built two country houses, which he lets furnished. They are by many degrees the best houses that are so let near our French watering-place; we have had the honour of living in both and can testify. The entrance-hall of the first we inhabited was ornamented with a plan of the estate, representing it as about twice the size of Ireland; insomuch that when we were yet new to the property (M. Loyal always speaks of it as 'La propriété') we went three miles straight on end in search of the bridge of Austerlitz – which we afterwards found to be immediately outside the window. The Château of the Old Guard, in another part of the grounds, and, according to the plan, about two leagues from the little dining-room, we sought in vain for a week, until, happening one evening to sit upon a bench in the forest (forest in the plan), a few yards from the house-door, we observed at our feet, in the ignominious circumstances of being upside down and greenly rotten, the Old Guard himself: that is to say, the painted effigy of a member of that distinguished corps, seven feet high, and in the act of carrying arms, who had had the misfortune to be blown down in the previous winter. It will be perceived that M. Loyal is a staunch admirer of the great Napoleon. He is an old soldier himself – captain of the National Guard, with a handsome gold vase on his chimney-piece, presented to him by his company – and his respect for the memory of the illustrious general is enthusiastic. Medallions of him, portraits of him, busts of him, pictures of him, are thickly sprinkled all over the property. During the first month of our occupation, it was our affliction to be constantly knocking

[92]

down Napoleon: if we touched a shelf in a dark corner, he toppled over with a crash; and every door we opened, shook him to the soul. Yet M. Loyal is not a man of mere castles in the air, or, as he would say, in Spain. He has a specially practical, contriving, clever, skilful eye and hand. His houses are delightful. He unites French elegance and English comfort, in a happy manner quite his own. He has an extraordinary genius for making tasteful little bedrooms in angles of his roofs, which an Englishman would as soon think of turning to any account as he would think of cultivating the Desert. We have ourself reposed deliciously in an elegant chamber of M. Loyal's construction, with our head as nearly in the kitchen chimney-pot as we can conceive it likely for the head of any gentleman, not by profession a Sweep, to be. And into whatsoever strange nook M. Loyal's genius penetrates, it, in that nook, infallibly constructs a cupboard and a row of pegs. In either of our houses, we could have put away the knapsacks and hung up the hats of the whole regiment of Guides.

Aforetime, M. Loyal was a tradesman in the town. You can transact business with no present tradesman in the town, and give your card 'chez M. Loyal,' but a brighter face shines upon you directly. We doubt if there is, ever was, or ever will be, a man so universally pleasant in the minds of people

[93]

as M. Loyal is in the minds of the citizens of our
French watering-place. They rub their hands and
laugh when they speak of him. Ah, but he is such a
good child, such a brave boy, such a generous
spirit, that Monsieur Loyal! It is the honest truth.
M. Loyal's nature is the nature of a gentleman. He
cultivates his ground with his own hands (assisted
by one little labourer, who falls into a fit now and
then); and he digs and delves from morn to eve in
prodigious perspirations – 'works always,' as he
says – but, cover him with dust, mud, weeds,
water, any stains you will, you never can cover the
gentleman in M. Loyal. A portly, upright, broad-
shouldered, brown faced man, whose soldierly
bearing gives him the appearance of being taller
than he is, look into the bright eye of M. Loyal,
standing before you in his working-blouse and cap,
not particularly well shaved, and, it may be, very
earthy, and you shall discern in M. Loyal a gentleman whose true politeness is in grain, and confirma-
tion of whose word by his bond you would blush to
think of. Not without reason is M. Loyal when he
tells that story, in his own vivacious way, of his
travelling to Fulham, near London, to buy all these
hundreds and hundreds of trees you now see upon
the Property, then a bare, bleak hill; and of his
sojourning in Fulham three months; and of his
jovial evenings with the market-gardeners; and of

[94]

the crowning banquet before his departure, when
the market-gardeners rose as one man, clinked their
glasses all together (as the custom at Fulham is),
and cried, 'Vive Loyal!'

M. Loyal has an agreeable wife, but no family;
and he loves to drill the children of his tenants, or
run races with them, or do anything with them, or
for them, that is good-natured. He is of a highly
convivial temperament, and his hospitality is un-
bounded. Billet a soldier on him, and he is delight-
ed. Five-and-thirty soldiers had M. Loyal billeted
on him this present summer, and they all got fat and
red-faced in two days. It became a legend among
the troops that whosoever got billeted on M. Loyal
rolled in clover; and so it fell out that the fortunate
man who drew the billet 'M. Loyal Devasseur'
always leaped into the air, though in heavy marching order. M. Loyal cannot bear to admit anything that might seem by any implication to dispa-
rage the military profession. We hinted to him
once, that we were conscious of a remote doubt
arising in our mind, whether a sou a day for
pocket-money, tobacco, stockings, drink, washing,
and social pleasures in general, left a very large
margin for a soldier's enjoyment. Pardon! said M.
Loyal, rather wincing. It was not a fortune, but – à
la bonne heure – it was better than it used to be!
What, we asked him on another occasion, were all

those neighbouring peasants, each living with his family in one room, and each having a soldier (perhaps two) billeted on him every other night, required to provide for those soldiers? 'Faith,' said M. Loyal, reluctantly; 'a bed, monsieur, and fire to cook with, and a candle. And they share their supper with those soldiers. It is not possible that they could eat alone.' – 'And what allowance do they get for this?' said we. Monsieur Loyal drew himself up taller, took a step back, laid his hand upon his breast, and said, with majesty, as speaking for himself and all France, 'Monsieur, it is a contribution to the State!'

It is never going to rain, according to M. Loyal. When it is impossible to deny that it is now raining in torrents, he says it will be fine – charming – magnificent – tomorrow. It is never hot on the Property, he contends. Likewise it is never cold. The flowers, he says, come out, delighting to grow there; it is like Paradise this morning; it is like the Garden of Eden. He is a little fanciful in his language: smilingly observing of Madame Loyal, when she is absent at vespers, that she is 'gone to her salvation' – allée à son salut. He has a great enjoyment of tobacco, but nothing would induce him to continue smoking face to face with a lady. His short black pipe immediately goes into his breast pocket, scorches his blouse, and nearly sets

him on fire. In the Town Council and on occasions
of ceremony, he appears in a full suit of black, with
a waistcoat of magnificent breadth across the chest,
and a shirt-collar of fabulous proportions. Good M.
Loyal! Under blouse or waistcoat, he carries one of
the gentlest hearts that beat in a nation teeming
with gentle people. He has had losses, and has been
at his best under them. Not only the loss of his way
by night in the Fulham times – when a bad subject
of an Englishman, under pretence of seeing him
home, took him into all the night public-houses,
drank 'arfanarf' in every one at his expense, and
finally fled, leaving him shipwrecked at Cleefeeway,
which we apprehend to be Ratcliffe Highway – but
heavier losses than that. Long ago a family of
children and a mother were left in one of his houses
without money, a whole year. M. Loyal – anything
but as rich as we wish he had been – had not the
heart to say 'you must go;' so they stayed on and
stayed on, and paying-tenants who would have
come in couldn't come in, and at last they managed
to get helped home across the water; and M. Loyal
kissed the whole group, and said, 'Adieu, my poor
infants!' and sat down in their deserted salon and
smoked his pipe of peace. – 'The rent, M. Loyal?'
'Eh! well! The rent!' M. Loyal shakes his head. 'Le
bon Dieu,' says M. Loyal presently, 'will recom-
pense me,' and he laughs and smokes his pipe of

[97]

peace. May he smoke it on the Property, and not be recompensed, these fifty years!

There are public amusements in our French watering-place, or it would not be French. They are very popular, and very cheap. The sea-bathing – which may rank as the most favoured daylight entertainment, inasmuch as the French visitors bathe all day long, and seldom appear to think of remaining less than an hour at a time in the water – is astoundingly cheap. Omnibuses convey you, if you please, from a convenient part of the town to the beach and back again; you have a clean and comfortable bathing-machine, dress, linen, and all appliances; and the charge for the whole is half-a-franc, or fivepence. On the pier, there is usually a guitar, which seems presumptuously enough to set its tinkling against the deep hoarseness of the sea, and there is always some boy or woman who sings, without any voice, little songs without any tune: the strain we have most frequently heard being an appeal to 'the sportsman' not to bag that choicest of game, the swallow. For bathing purposes, we have also a subscription establishment with an esplanade, where people lounge about with telescopes, and seem to get a good deal of weariness for their money; and we have also an association of individual machine proprietors combined against this formidable rival. M. Féroce, our own particular friend in the bathing line, is one of these. He is as gentle and polite a man as M. Loyal Devasseur himself; immensely stout withal, and of a beaming aspect. M. Féroce has saved so many people from drowning, and has been decorated with so many medals in consequence, that his stoutness seems a special dispensation of Providence to enable him to wear them; if his girth were the girth of an ordinary man, he could never hang them on, all at once. It is only on very great occasions that M. Féroce displays his shining honours. At other times they lie by, with rolls of manuscript testifying to the causes of their presentation, in a huge glass case in the red-sofa'd salon of his private residence on the beach, where M. Féroce also keeps his family pictures, his portraits of himself as he appears both in bathing life and in private life, his little boats that rock by clockwork, and his other ornamental possessions.

Then, we have a commodious and gay Theatre – or had, for it is burned down now – where the opera was always preceded by a vaudeville, in which (as usual) everybody, down to the little old man with the large hat and the little cane and tassel, who always played either my Uncle or my Papa, suddenly broke out of the dialogue into the mildest vocal snatches, to the great perplexity of unaccustomed strangers from Great Britain, who never could make out when they were singing and when they were talking – and indeed it was pretty much the same. But the caterers in the way of entertainment to whom we are most beholden are the Society of Welldoing, who are active all the summer, and give the proceeds of their good works to the poor. Some of the most agreeable fêtes they contrive are announced as 'Dedicated to the children;' and the taste with which they turn a small public enclosure into an elegant garden beautifully illuminated, and the thorough-going heartiness and energy with which they personally direct the childish pleasures, are supremely delightful. For fivepence a head, we have on these occasions donkey races with English 'Jokeis,' and other rustic sports; lotteries for toys, roundabouts, dancing on the grass to the music of an admirable band, fire-balloons and fireworks. Further, almost every week all through the summer – never mind, now, on what day of the week – there is a fête in some adjoining village (called in that part of the country a Ducasse), where the people – really *the people* – dance on the green turf in the open air, round a little orchestra, that seems itself to dance, there is such an airy motion of flags and streamers about it. And we do not suppose that between the Torrid Zone and the North Pole there are to be found male dancers with such astonishingly loose legs, furnished with so many joints in wrong places, utterly unknown to Professor Owen, as those who

[100]

here disport themselves. Sometimes the fête apper-
tains to a particular trade; you will see among the
cheerful young women at the joint Ducasse of the
milliners and tailors, a wholesome knowledge of the
art of making common and cheap things uncommon
and pretty, by good sense and good taste, that is a
practical lesson to any rank of society in a whole
island we could mention. The oddest feature of
these agreeable scenes is the everlasting Round-
about (we preserve an English word wherever we
can; as we are writing the English language), on the
wooden-horses of which machine grown-up people
of all ages are wound round and round with the
utmost solemnity, while the proprietor's wife grinds
an organ, capable of only one tune, in the centre.

As to the boarding-houses of our French
watering-place, they are Legion, and would require
a distinct treatise. It is not without a sentiment of
national pride that we believe them to contain more
bores from the shores of Albion than all the clubs in
London. As you walk timidly in their neighbourhood, the very neckcloths and hats of your elderly
compatriots cry to you from the stones of the
streets, 'We are Bores – avoid us!' We have never
overheard at street corners such lunatic scraps of
political and social discussion as among these dear
countrymen of ours. They believe everything that is
impossible and nothing that is true. They carry

rumours, and ask questions, and make corrections and improvements to one another, staggering to the human intellect. And they are for ever rushing into the English library, propounding such incomprehensible paradoxes to the fair mistress of that establishment, that we beg to recommend her to her Majesty's gracious consideration as a fit object for a pension.

The English form a considerable part of the population of our French watering-place, and are deservedly addressed and respected in many ways. Some of the surface-addresses to them are odd enough, as when a laundress puts a placard outside her house announcing her possession of that curious British instrument, a 'Mingle;' or when a tavern-keeper provides accommodation for the celebrated English game of 'Nokemdon.' But, to us, it is not the least pleasant feature of our French watering-place that a long and constant fusion of the two great nations there has taught each to like the other, and to learn from the other, and to rise superior to the absurd prejudices that have lingered among the weak and ignorant in both countries equally.

Drumming and trumpeting of course go on for ever in our French watering-place. Flag-flying is at a premium too; but we cheerfully avow that we consider a flag a very pretty object, and that we take such outward signs of innocent liveliness to our heart of hearts. The people in the town and in the country, are a busy people who work hard; they are sober, temperate, good-humoured, light-hearted, and generally remarkable for their engaging manners. Few just men, not immoderately bilious, could see them in their recreations without very much respecting the character that is so easily, so harmlessly, and so simply, pleased.

TRAVELLING ABROAD

(from The Uncommercial Traveller)

'Whenever I am in Paris, I am dragged by invisible force into the Morgue. I never want to go there, but am always pulled there.'

I got into the travelling chariot – it was of German make, roomy, heavy, and unvarnished – I got into the travelling chariot, pulled up the steps after me, shut myself in with a smart bang of the door, and gave the word, 'Go on!'

Immediately, all that W. and S.W. division of London began to slide away at a pace so lively, that I was over the river and past the Old Kent Road, and out on Blackheath, and even ascending Shooter's Hill, before I had time to look about me in the carriage, like a collected traveller.

I had two ample Imperials on the roof, other fitted storage for luggage in front, and other up behind; I had a net for books overhead, great pockets to all the windows, a leathern lamp fixed in the back of the chariot, in case I should be benighted. I was amply provided in all respects, and had no idea where I was going (which was delightful), except that I was going abroad.

[104]

So smooth was the old high road, and so fresh were the horses, and so fast went I, that it was midway between Gravesend and Rochester, and the widening river was bearing the ships, white-sailed or black-smoked, out to sea, when I noticed by the wayside a very queer small boy.

'Holloa!' said I, to the very queer small boy, 'where do you live?'

'At Chatham,' says he.

'What do you do there?' says I.

'I go to school,' says he.

I took him up in a moment, and we went on. Presently, the very queer small boy says, 'This is Gads-hill we are coming to, where Falstaff went out to rob those travellers, and ran away.'

'You know something about Falstaff, eh?' said I.

'All about him,' said the very queer small boy. 'I am old (I am nine), and I read all sorts of books. But *do* let us stop at the top of the hill, and look at the house there, if you please!'

'You admire that house?' said I.

'Bless you, sir,' said the very queer small boy, 'when I was not more than half as old as nine, it used to be a treat for me to be brought to look at it. And now, I am nine, I come by myself to look at it. And ever since I can recollect, my father, seeing me so fond of it, has often said to me, "If you were to be very persevering and were to work hard, you might

[105]

some day come to live in it." Though that's impossible!' said the very queer small boy, drawing a low breath, and now staring at the house out of window with all his might.

I was rather amazed to be told this by the very queer small boy; for that house happens to be *my* house, and I have reason to believe that what he said was true.

Well! I made no halt there, and I soon dropped the very queer small boy and went on. Over the road where the old Romans used to march, over the road where the old Canterbury pilgrims used to go, over the road where the travelling trains of the old imperious priests and princes used to jingle on horseback between the continent and this Island through the mud and water, over the road where Shakespeare hummed to himself, 'Blow, blow, thou winter wind,' as he sat in the saddle at the gate of the inn yard noticing the carriers; all among the cherry orchards, apple orchards, corn-fields, and hop-gardens; so went I, by Canterbury to Dover. There, the sea was tumbling in, with deep sounds, after dark, and the revolving French light on Cape Grinez was seen regularly bursting out and becoming obscured, as if the head of a gigantic light-keeper in an anxious state of mind were inter-posed every half-minute, to look how it was burning.

Early in the morning I was on the deck of the

steam-packet, and we were aiming at the bar in the usual intolerable manner, and the bar was aiming at us in the usual intolerable manner, and the bar got by far the best of it, and we got by far the worst – all in the usual intolerable manner.

But, when I was clear of the Custom House on the other side, and when I began to make the dust fly on the thirsty French roads, and when the twigsome trees by the wayside (which, I suppose, never will grow leafy, for they never did) guarded here and there a dusty soldier, or field labourer, baking on a heap of broken stones, sound asleep in a fiction of shade, I began to recover my travelling spirits. Coming upon the breaker of the broken stones, in a hard hot shining hat, on which the sun played at a distance as on a burning-glass, I felt that now, indeed, I was in the dear old France of my affections. I should have known it, without the well-remembered bottle of rough ordinary wine, the cold roast fowl, the loaf, and the pinch of salt, on which I lunched with unspeakable satisfaction, from one of the stuffed pockets of the chariot.

I must have fallen asleep after lunch, for when a bright face looked in at the window, I started and said:

'Good God, Louis, I dreamed you were dead!'

My cheerful servant laughed, and answered:

'Me? Not at all, sir.'

'How glad I am to wake! What are we doing, Louis?'

'We go to take relay of horses. Will you walk up the hill?'

'Certainly.'

Welcome the old French hill, with the old French lunatic (not in the most distant degree related to Sterne's Maria) living in a thatched dog-kennel half-way up, and flying out with his crutch and his big head and extended nightcap, to be beforehand with the old men and women exhibiting crippled children, and with the children exhibiting old men and women, ugly and blind, who always seemed by resurrectionary process to be recalled out of the elements for the sudden peopling of the solitude!

'It is well,' said I, scattering among them what small coin I had; 'here comes Louis, and I am quite roused from my nap.'

We journeyed on again, and I welcomed every new assurance that France stood where I had left it. There were the posting-houses, with their arch-ways, dirty stable-yards, and clean postmasters' wives, bright women of business, looking on at the putting-to of the horses; there were the postilions counting what money they got, into their hats, and never making enough of it; there were the standard population of grey horses of Flanders descent, invariably biting one another when they got a

chance; there were the fleecy sheepskins, looped on
over their uniforms by the postilions, like bibbed
aprons when it blew and rained; there were their
jack-boots, and their cracking whips; there were the
cathedrals that I got out to see, as under some cruel
bondage, in no wise desiring to see them; there were
the little towns that appeared to have no reason for
being towns, since most of their houses were to let
and nobody could be induced to look at them,
except the people who wouldn't let them and had
nothing else to do but look at them all day. I lay a
night upon the road and enjoyed delectable cookery
of potatoes, and some other sensible things, adop-
tion of which at home would inevitably be shown to
be fraught with ruin, somehow or other, to that
rickety national blessing, the British farmer; and at
last I was rattled, like a single pill in a box, over
leagues of stones, until – madly cracking, plunging,
and flourishing two grey tails about – I made my
triumphal entry into Paris.

At Paris, I took an upper apartment for a few
days in one of the hotels of the Rue de Rivoli; my
front windows looking into the garden of the
Tuileries (where the principal difference between
the nursemaids and the flowers seemed to be that
the former were locomotive and the latter not): my
back windows looking at all the other back windows
in the hotel, and deep down into a paved yard,

[109]

where my German chariot had retired under a
tight-fitting archway, to all appearance for life, and
where bells rang all day without anybody's minding
them but certain chamberlains with feather brooms
and green baize caps, who here and there leaned out
of some high window placidly looking down, and
where neat waiters with trays on their left shoulders
passed and repassed from morning to night.

Whenever I am in Paris, I am dragged by invisible force into the Morgue. I never want to go there,
but am always pulled there. One Christmas Day,
when I would rather have been anywhere else, I was
attracted in, to see an old grey man lying all alone
on his cold bed, with a tap of water turned on over
his grey hair, and running, drip, drip, drip, down
his wretched face until it go to the corner of his
mouth, where it took a turn, and made him look
sly. One New Year's Morning (by the same token,
the sun was shining outside, and there was a
mountebank balancing a feather on his nose, within
a yard of the gate), I was pulled in again to look at a
flaxen-haired boy of eighteen, with a heart hanging
on his breast – 'from his mother,' was engraven on
it – who had come into the net across the river, with
a bullet wound in his fair forehead and his hands cut
with a knife, but whence or how was a blank
mystery. This time, I was forced into the same
dread place, to see a large dark man whose dis-

figurement by water was in a frightful manner comic, and whose expression was that of a prize-fighter who had closed his eyelids under a heavy blow, but was going immediately to open them, shake his head, and 'come up smiling.' O what this large dark man cost me in that bright city!

It was very hot weather, and he was none the better for that, and I was much the worse. Indeed, a very neat and pleasant little woman with the key of her lodging on her forefinger, who had been showing him to her little girl while she and the child ate sweetmeats, observed monsieur looking poorly as we came out together, and asked monsieur, with her wondering little eyebrows prettily raised, if there were anything the matter? Faintly replying in the negative, monsieur crossed the road to a wine-shop, got some brandy and resolved to freshen himself with a dip in the great floating bath on the river.

The bath was crowded in the usual airy manner, by a male population in striped drawers of various gay colours, who walked up and down arm in arm, drank coffee, smoked cigars, sat at little tables, conversed politely with the damsels who dispensed the towels, and every now and then pitched themselves into the river head foremost, and came out again to repeat this social routine. I made haste to participate in the water part of the entertainments, and was in the full enjoyment of a delightful bath, when all in a moment I was seized by an unreasonable idea that the large dark body was floating straight at me.

I was out of the river and dressing instantly. In the shock I had taken some water into my mouth, and it turned me sick, for I fancied that the contamination of the creature was in it. I had got back to my cool darkened room in the hotel, and was lying on a sofa there, before I began to reason with myself.

Of course, I knew perfectly well that the large dark creature was stone dead, and that I should no more come upon him out of the place where I had seen him dead, than I should come upon the cathedral of Notre-Dame in an entirely new situation. What troubled me was the picture of the creature; and that had so curiously and strongly painted itself upon my brain, that I could not get rid of it until it was worn out.

I noticed the peculiarities of this possession, while it was a real discomfort to me. That very day, at dinner, some morsel on my plate looked like a piece of him, and I was glad to get up and go out. Later in the evening, I was walking along the Rue St. Honoré, when I saw a bill at a public room there, announcing small-sword exercise, broadsword exercise, wrestling and other such feats. I went in, and some of the sword-play being very skilful, remained. A specimen of our own national sport, The British Boaxe, was announced to be given at the close of the evening. In an evil hour, I determined to wait for this Boaxe, as became a Briton. It was a clumsy specimen (executed by two English grooms out of place), but one of the combatants, receiving a straight right-hander with the glove between his eyes, did exactly what the large dark creature in the Morgue had seemed going to do – and finished me for that night.

There was a rather sickly smell (not at all an unusual fragrance in Paris) in the little ante-room of my apartment at the hotel. The large dark creature in the Morgue was by no direct experience associated with my sense of smell, because, when I came to the knowledge of him, he lay behind a wall of thick plate-glass as good as a wall of steel or marble for that matter. Yet the whiff of the room never failed to reproduce him. What was more curious, was the capriciousness with which his portrait seemed to light itself up in my mind, elsewhere. I might be walking in the Palais Royal, lazily enjoying the shop windows, and might be regaling myself with one of the ready-made clothes shops that are set out there. My eyes, wandering over impossible-waisted dressing-gowns and luminous waistcoats, would fall upon the master, or the shopman, or even the very dummy at the door, and would suggest to me, 'Something like him!' – and instantly I was sickened again.

This would happen at the theatre, in the same manner. Often it would happen in the street, when I certainly was not looking for the likeness, and when probably there was no likeness there. It was not because the creature was dead that I was so haunted, because I know that I might have been (and I know it because I have been) equally attended by the image of a living aversion. This lasted about a week. The picture did not fade by degrees, in the sense that it became a whit less forcible and distinct, but in the sense that it obtruded itself less and less frequently. The experience may be worth considering by some who have the care of children. It would be difficult to overstate the intensity and accuracy of an intelligent child's observation. At that impressible time of life, it must sometimes produce a fixed impression. If the fixed impression be of an object terrible to the child, it will be (for want of reasoning upon) inseparable from great fear. Force the child at such a time, be Spartan with it, send it into the dark against its will, leave it in a lonely bedroom against its will, and you had better murder it.

On a bright morning I rattled away from Paris, in the German chariot, and left the dark creature behind me for good. I ought to confess, though, that I had been drawn back to the Morgue, after he was put underground, to look at his clothes, and that I found them frightfully like him – particularly his boots. However, I rattled away for Switzerland, looking forward and not backward, and so we parted company.

[*Editor's note:* In the remainder of this essay, the Uncommercial Traveller journeys on to Strasbourg and Switzerland.]

Extracts From Correspondence

From a letter to John Forster dated 26 June 1853, describing Boulogne, his villa there and the landlord, M. Beaucourt, who is portrayed as M. Loyal Devasseur in 'Our French Watering-Place' (see pp 80–103)

. . . O the rain here yesterday! A great sea-fog rolling in, a strong wind blowing, and the rain coming down in torrents all day long . . . This house is on a great hill-side, backed up by woods of young trees. It faces the Haute Ville with the ramparts and the unfinished cathedral – which capital object is exactly opposite the windows. On the slope in front, going steep down to the right, all Boulogne is piled and jumbled about in a very picturesque manner. The view is charming – closed in at least by the tops of swelling hills; and the door is within ten minutes of the post-office, and within quarter of an hour of the sea. The garden is made in terraces up the hill-side, like an Italian garden; the top walks being in the before-mentioned woods. The best part of it begins at the level of the house, and goes up at the back, a couple of hundred feet perhaps. There are at present thousands of roses all about the house, and no end of other flowers. There are five great summer-houses, and (I think) fifteen fountains – not one of which (according to the

[116]

invariable French custom) ever plays. The house is a doll's house of many rooms. It is one story high, with eight and thirty steps up and down – tribune wise – to the front door; the noblest French demonstration I have ever seen I think. It is a double house; and as there are only four windows and a pigeon-hole to be beheld in the front, you would suppose it to contain about four rooms. Being built on the hill-side, the top story of the house at the back – there are two stories there – opens on the level of another garden. On the ground floor there is a very pretty hall, almost all glass; a little dining room opening on a beautiful conservatory, which is also looked into through a great transparent glass in a mirror-frame over the chimney piece, just as in Paxton's room at Chatsworth; a spare bed-room, two little drawing-rooms opening into another, the family bed-rooms, a bath-room, a glass corridor, an open yard, and a kind of kitchen with a machinery of stoves and boilers. Above, there are eight tiny bed-rooms all opening on one great room in the roof, originally intended for a billiard-room. In the basement there is an admirable kitchen with every conceivable requisite in it, a noble cellar, first-rate man's room and pantry; coach-house, stable, coal-store and wood-store; and in the garden is a pavilion, containing an excellent spare bed-room on the ground floor. The getting-up of these places, the

[117]

looking-glasses, clocks, little stoves, all manner of
fittings, must be seen to be appreciated. The conservatory is full of choice flowers and perfectly
beautiful . . .

But the landlord – M. Beaucourt – is wonderful.
Everybody here has two surnames (I cannot conceive why), and M. Beaucourt, as he is always
called, is by rights M. Beaucourt-Mutuel. He is a
portly jolly fellow with a fine open face; lives on the
hill behind, just outside the top of the garden; and
was a linen draper in the town, where he still has a
shop, but is supposed to have mortgaged his business and to be in difficulties – all along of this place,
which he has planted with his own hands; which he
cultivates all day; and which he never on any
consideration speaks of but as 'the property.' He is
extraordinarily popular in Boulogne (the people in
the shops invariably brightening up at the mention
of his name, and congratulating us on being his
tenants), and really seems to deserve it. He is such a
liberal fellow that I can't bear to ask him for
anything, since he instantly supplies it whatever it
is. The things he has done in respect of unreasonable bedsteads and washing-stands, I blush to think
of. I observed the other day in one of the side
gardens – there are gardens at each side of the house
too – a place where I thought the Comic Country-
man[1] must infallibly trip over, and make a little

[118]

descent of a dozen feet. So I said 'M. Beaucourt' –
who instantly pulled off his cap and stood
bareheaded – 'there are some space pieces of wood
lying by the cowhouse, if you would have the
kindness to have one laid across here I think it
would be safer.' 'Ah, mon dieu sir,' said M.
Beaucourt, 'it must be iron. This is not a portion of
the property where you would like to see wood.'
'But iron is so expensive,' said I, 'and it really is not
worth while –' 'Sir, pardon me a thousand times,'
said M. Beaucourt, 'it shall be iron. Assuredly and
perfectly it shall be iron.' 'Then M. Beaucourt,'
said I, 'I shall be glad to pay a moiety of the cost.'
'Sir,' said M. Beaucourt, 'Never!' Then to change
the subject, he slided from his firmness and gravity
into a graceful conversational tone, and said, 'In the
moonlight last night, the flowers on the property
appeared, O Heaven, to be *bathing themselves in the
sky*. You like the property?' 'M. Beaucourt,' said I,
'I am enchanted with it; I am more than satisfied
with everything.' 'And I sir,' said M. Beaucourt,
laying his cap upon his breast, and kissing his hand
– 'I equally!' Yesterday two blacksmiths came for a
day's work, and put up a good solid handsome bit of
iron-railing, morticed into the stone parapet . . . If
the extraordinary things in the house defy description, the amazing phenomena in the gardens never
could have been dreamed of by anybody but a

[119]

Frenchman bent upon one idea. Besides a portrait of the house in the dining-room, there is a plan of the property in the hall. It looks about the size of Ireland; and to every one of the extraordinary objects, there is a reference with some portentous name. There are fifty-one such references, including the Cottage of Tom Thumb, the Bridge of Austerlitz, the Bridge of Jena, the Hermitage, the Bower of the Old Guard, the Labyrinth (I have no idea which is which); and there is guidance to every room in the house, as if it were a place on that stupendous scale that without such a clue you must infallibly lose your way, and perhaps perish of starvation between bedroom and bedroom. . . .

[1] His nickname for his youngest son, then 1¼ years old.

☆　☆　☆　☆　☆

From a letter to W.H. Wills dated 21 October 1855, describing his apartment in Paris at 49 avenue des Champs-Élysées

I have two floors here – entresol and first – in a Doll's house, but really pretty within, and the view without, astounding – as you will say when you come. The House is on the Exposition side, about half a quarter of a mile above Franconi's, of course on the other side of the way, and close to the Jardin d'Hiver. Each room has but one window in it, but we have no fewer than six rooms (besides the back ones) looking on the Champs Elysées, with the wonderful life perpetually flowing up and down. We have no spare-room, but excellent stowage for the whole family, including a capital dressing room for me, and a really slap-up Kitchen near the stars! Damage for the whole, 700 francs a month.

But Sir – but – when Georgina, the servants, and I, were here for the first night (Catherine and the rest being at Boulogne), I heard Georgy restless – turned out – asked 'What's the matter?' – 'Oh it's dreadfully dirty. I can't sleep for the smell of my room.' Imagine all my stage-managerial energies multiplied, at daybreak by 1,000. Imagine the porter, the porter's wife, the porter's wife's sister, a feeble upholsterer of enormous age from round the corner, and all his workmen (4 boys) summoned. Imagine the partners in the proprietorship of the apartment – old lady, and martial little man with François Premier beard – also summoned. Imagine your inimitable chief briefly explaining that Dirt is not in his way, and that he is driven to madness, and that he devotes himself to no coat and a dirty face until the apartment is thoroughly purified. Imagine co-proprietors at first astounded – then urging that 'it's not the custom' – then wavering – then affected – then confiding their utmost private sorrows to the Inimitable – offering new carpets (accepted), embraces (not accepted), and really responding like French Bricks. Sallow, unbrushed, unshorn, awful, stalks the Inimitable through the apartment until last night. Then all the improvements were concluded, and I do really believe the place to be now worth 800 or 900 francs per month. You must picture it as the smallest place you ever saw, but as exquisitely cheerful and vivacious – clean as anything human can be – and with a moving panorama always outside, which is Paris in itself.

From a letter to John Forster, dated 30 January 1856, on translation rights, rain in the Champs-Élysées, and military bands

. . . I have arranged with the French bookselling house to receive, by monthly payments of £40, the sum of £440 for the right to translate all my books: that is, what they call my Romances, and what I call my Stories. This does not include the Christmas

Books, American Notes, Pictures from Italy, or the Sketches; but they are to have the right to translate them for extra payments if they choose. In consideration of this venture as to the unprotected property, I cede them the right of translating all future Romances at a thousand francs (£40) each. Considering that I get so much for what is otherwise worth nothing, and get my books before so clever and important a people, I think this is not a bad move? . . .

. . . It is surprising what a change nine years have made in my notoriety here. So many of the rising French generation now read English (and Chuzzlewit is now being translated daily in the Moniteur), that I can't go into a shop and give my card without being acknowledged in the pleasantest way possible. A curiosity-dealer brought home some little knick-knacks I had bought, the other night, and knew all my books from beginning to end of 'em. There is much of the personal friendliness in my readers, here, that is so delightful at home; and I have been greatly surprised and pleased by the unexpected discovery. . .

. . . We have wet weather here – and dark too for these latitudes – and oceans of mud. Although numbers of men are perpetually scooping and sweeping it away in this thoroughfare, it accumulates under the windows so fast, and in such sludgy

[123]

masses, that to get across the road is to get half over one's shoes in the first outset of a walk . . . It is difficult to picture the change made in this place by the removal of the paving stones (too ready for barricades), and macadamization. It suits neither climate nor the soil. We are again in a sea of mud. One cannot cross the road of the Champs Elysées here, without being half over one's boots . . . Three days ago the weather changed here in an hour, and we have had bright weather and hard frost ever since. All the mud disappeared with marvellous rapidity, and the sky became Italian. Taking advantage of such a happy change, I started off yesterday morning (for exercise and meditation) on a scheme I have taken into my head, to walk round the walls of Paris. It is a very odd walk, and will make a good description. Yesterday I turned to the right when I got outside the Barrière de l'Etoile, walked round the wall till I came to the river, and then entered Paris beyond the site of the Bastille. To-day I mean to turn to the left when I get outside the Barrière, and see what comes of that . . .

. . . It was cold this afternoon, as bright as Italy, and these Elysian Fields crowded with carriages, riders, and foot passengers. All the fountains were playing, all the Heavens shining. Just as I went out at 4 o'clock, several regiments that had passed out at the Barrière in the morning to exercise in the country, came marching back, in the straggling French manner, which is far more picturesque and real than anything you can imagine in that way. Alternately great storms of drums played, and then the most delicious and skilful bands, Trovatore music, Barber of Seville, music, all sorts of music with well-marked melody and time. All bloused Paris (led by the Inimitable, and a poor cripple who works himself up and down all day in a big-wheeled car) went at a quick march down the avenue, in a sort of hilarious dance. If the colours with the golden eagle on the top had only been unfurled, we should have followed them anywhere, in any cause – much as the children follow Punches in the better cause of Comedy. Napoleon on the top of the Column seemed up to the whole thing, I thought.

. . . I have a grim pleasure upon me to-night in thinking that the Circumlocution Office sees the light, and in wondering what effect it will make. But my head really stings with the visions of the book, and I am going, as we French say, to dis-embarrass it by plunging out into some of the strange places I glide into of nights in these latitudes . . .

Extracts from Correspondence

*Letter to Wilkie Collins dated 22 April 1856, on,
among other things, a not-so-successful Parisian pro-
duction of As You Like It and dinner with the press
entrepreneur and literary and political celebrity Émile
de Girardin*

My Dear Collins, – I have been quite taken aback
by your account of your alarming seizure; and have
only become reassured again, firstly by the good
fortune of your having left here and got so near your
doctor; secondly, by your hopefulness of now making head in the right direction. On the 3rd or 4th I
propose being in town, and I need not say that I
shall forthwith come to look after my old Patient.

On Sunday, to my infinite amazement, Townshend appeared. He has changed his plans, and is
staying in Paris a week, before going to Town for a
couple of months. He dined here on Sunday, and
placidly ate and drank in the most vigorous manner,
and mildly laid out a terrific perspective of projects
for carrying me off to the Theatre every night. But
in the morning he found himself with dawnings of
Bronchitis, and is now luxuriously laid up in laven-
der at his Hotel – confining himself entirely to
precious stones, chicken, and fragrant wines qualified with iced waters.

Last Friday I took Mrs. Dickens, Georgina, and
Mary and Katey, to dine at the Trois Frères. We
then, sir, went off to the Français to see Comme il

[126]

vous plaira – which is a kind of Theatrical Representation that I think might be got up, with great completeness, by the Patients in the asylum for Idiots. Dreariness is no word for it, vacancy is no word for it, gammon is no word for it, there *is* no word for it. Nobody has anything to do but to sit upon as many grey stones as he can. When Jacques had sat upon seventy-seven stones and forty-two roots of trees (which was at the end of the second act), we came away. He had by that time been made violent love to by Celia, had shown himself in every phase of his existence to be utterly unknown to Shakespeare, had made the speech about the Seven Ages out of its right place, and apropos of nothing on earth, and had in all respects conducted himself like a brutalized, benighted, and besotted Beast.

A wonderful dinner at Girardin's last Monday, with only one new (but appropriate) feature in it. When we went into the drawing-room after the banquet, which had terminated in a flower-pot out of a ballet being set before every guest, piled to the brim with the ruddiest fresh strawberries, he asked me if I would come into another room (a chamber of no account – rather like the last Scene in Gustavus) and smoke a cigar. On my replying yes, he opened with a key attached to his watch-chain, a species of mahogany cave, which appeared to me to extend under the Champs Elysées, and in which were piled

[127]

about four hundred thousand inestimable and un-
attainable cigars, in bundles or bales of about a
thousand each.

Yesterday I dined at the bookseller's with the
body of Translators engaged on my new Edition –
one of them a lady, young and pretty. (I hope,
by-the-bye, judging from the questions which they
asked me and which I asked them, that it will be
really well done.). Among them was an extremely
amiable old Savant, who occasionally expressed
himself in a foreign tongue which I supposed to be
Russian (I thought he had something to do with the
congress perhaps), but which my host told me,
when I came away, was English! We wallowed in an
odd sort of dinner, which would have been splashy
if it hadn't been too sticky. Salmon appeared late in
the evening, and unforeseen creatures of the lobster
species strayed in after the pudding. It was very
hospitable and good-natured though, and we all got
on in the friendliest way. Please to imagine me for
three mortal hours incessantly holding forth to the
translators, and, among other things, addressing
them in a neat and appropriate (French) speech. I
came home quite light-headed.

On Saturday night I paid three francs at the door
of that place where we saw the wrestling, and went
in, at 11 o'clock, to a Ball. Much the same as our
own National Argyll Rooms. Some pretty faces, but

[128]

all of two classes – wicked and coldly calculating, or haggard and wretched in their worn beauty. Among the latter was a woman of thirty or so, in an Indian shawl, who never stirred from a seat in a corner all the time I was there. Handsome, regardless, brooding, and yet with some nobler qualities in her forehead. I mean to walk about to-night and look for her. I didn't speak to her there, but I have a fancy that I should like to know more about her. Never shall, I suppose.

Franconi's I have been to again, of course. Nowhere else. I finished 'that' No. as soon as Macready went away, and have done something for Household Words next week, called Proposals for a National Jest Book, that I take rather kindly to. The first blank page of Little Dorrit, No. 8, now eyes me on this desk with a pressing curiosity. It will get nothing out of me to-day, I distinctly perceive.

Townshend's Henri and Bully (the dog) have just been here – came in with a message at the double dash – The Bully disconcerted me a good deal. He dined here on Sunday with his master, and got a young family of puppies out of each of the doors, fell into indecent transports with the claw of the round table, and was madly in love with Townshend's boots, all of which Townshend seems to have no idea of, but merely says – 'Bul-la!' when he is on his hind legs like the sign of a public house.

If he dines here again, I mean to have a trifle of camphor ready for him, and to try whether it has the effect upon him that it is said to have upon the Monks (with which piece of scientific knowledge I taunt Stanfield when we go out together).

That swearing of the Academy Carpenters is the best thing of its kind I ever heard of. I suppose the oath to be administered by little Knight. It's my belief that the stout Porter, now no more, wouldn't have taken it. Our cook's going. Says she 'ain't strong enough for BooLone.' I don't know what there is particularly trying in that climate. The nice little Nurse, who goes into all manner of shops without knowing one word of French, took some lace to be mended the other day, and the Shop-keeper, impressed with the idea that she had come to sell it, *would* give her money; with which she returned weeping, believing it (until explanation ensued) to be the price of shame.

All send kindest regard. – Ever faithfully.

*From a letter to W.H. Wills dated 4 February 1863,
on the audience reaction to his readings in Paris*

It is really the general Parisian impression that such a hit was never made here. The curiosity and interest and general buzz about it are quite indescribable. They are so extraordinarily quick to understand a face and gesture, going together, that one of the remarkable points is, that people who don't understand English, positively understand the Readings! I suppose that such an audience for a piece of Art is not to be found in the world. I wish you could have seen them – firstly, for my effect upon them – secondly, for their effect upon me. You have no idea what they made of me. I got things out of the old Carol – effects I mean – so entirely new and so very strong, that I quite amazed myself and wondered where I was going next. I really listened to Mr. Peggotty's narrative in Copperfield, with admiration. When Little Emily's letter was read, a low murmur of irrepressible emotion went about like a sort of sea. When Steerforth made a pause in shaking hands with Ham, they all lighted up as if the notion fired an electric chain. When David proposed to Dora, gorgeous beauties all radiant with diamonds, clasped their fans between their two hands, and rolled about in ecstasy. They took the storm as if

[131]

they were in it. As to the Trial, their perception of the Witnesses, and particularly of Mr. Winkle, was quite extraordinary. And whenever they saw the old Judge coming in, they tapped one another and laughed with that amazing relish that I could hardly help laughing as much myself. All this culminated on the last night, when they positively applauded and called out expressions of delight, out of the room into the cloak room, out of the cloak room into their carriages, and in their carriages away down the Faubourg.

Of course, if I had gone on, I could have made a great deal of money. But I thought the dignified course was to stop. I could not reconcile myself to the notion of making the charitable help, the stepping-stone. So, for the present, I have done here.